THE TACO TUESDAY COOKBOOK
Plant-Based

THE TACO TUESDAY COOKBOOK
Plant-Based

KATE KASBEE
author of *Vegan Boards*

52 HEALTHY VEGAN TACO DINNERS FOR ANY WEEK OF THE YEAR

Quarto.com

© 2025 Quarto Publishing Group USA Inc.
Text © 2025 Kate Pelletier

First Published in 2025 by The Harvard Common Press, an imprint of The Quarto Group, 100 Cummings Center, Suite 265-D, Beverly, MA 01915, USA. T (978) 282-9590 F (978) 283-2742

All rights reserved. No part of this book may be reproduced in any form without written permission of the copyright owners. All images in this book have been reproduced with the knowledge and prior consent of the artists concerned, and no responsibility is accepted by producer, publisher, or printer for any infringement of copyright or otherwise, arising from the contents of this publication. Every effort has been made to ensure that credits accurately comply with the information supplied. We apologize for any inaccuracies that may have occurred and will resolve inaccurate or missing information in a subsequent reprinting of the book.

The Harvard Common Press titles are also available at discount for retail, wholesale, promotional, and bulk purchase. For details, contact the Special Sales Manager by email at specialsales@quarto.com or by mail at The Quarto Group, Attn: Special Sales Manager, 100 Cummings Center, Suite 265-D, Beverly, MA 01915, USA.

29 28 27 26 25   1 2 3 4 5

ISBN: 978-0-7603-9705-3

Digital edition published in 2025
eISBN: 978-0-7603-9706-0

Library of Congress Cataloging-in-Publication Data
Names: Kasbee, Kate author
Title: The taco Tuesday cookbook : 52 healthy vegan taco dinners for any week of the year / Kate Kasbee.
Description: Plant-based. | Beverly, MA, USA : Harvard Common Press, 2025. | Includes index.
Identifiers: LCCN 2025006020 (print) | LCCN 2025006021 (ebook) | ISBN
    9780760397053 trade paperback | ISBN 9780760397060 ebook
Subjects: LCSH: Vegan cooking | Tacos | Dinners and dining | LCGFT: Cookbooks
Classification: LCC TX837 .K25629 2025 (print) | LCC TX837 (ebook) | DDC
    41.84--dc23/eng/20250227
LC record available at https://lccn.loc.gov/2025006020
LC ebook record available at https://lccn.loc.gov/2025006021

Design and Page Layout: Samantha J. Bednarek, samanthabednarek.com
Photography: Kate Pelletier, except Amanda Farmer on page 150

Printed in China

**FOR JUNE, MY TINY GIRL
WITH A BIG APPETITE**

CONTENTS

INTRODUCTION: MAKING TACO TUESDAY VEGAN ... 9

CHAPTER 1
THE BASICS: TORTILLAS, SALSAS, SAUCES ... 15

Corn Tortillas ... **16**
Flour Tortillas ... **19**
Guacamole ... **20**
Salsa Verde ... **21**
Salsa Roja ... **23**
Cashew Queso ... **24**
Chipotle Aioli ... **26**
Pickled Red Onion ... **27**
Mango Salsa ... **29**
Jalapeño Ranch ... **30**

CHAPTER 2
VEGAN CHEESY TACOS ... 33

Crispy Black Bean and Cashew Queso Tacos ... **34**
Cheesy Smashburger Tacos ... **37**
Chile Relleno–Style Tacos ... **38**
Jalapeño Popper Taquitos ... **41**
Loaded Tater Tot Tacos ... **42**
Cheesy Potato Tacos ... **45**
Cheesy and Crunchy Vegan Gorditas ... **46**
Cheesy Bean and Rice Taquitos ... **49**

CHAPTER 3
BEAN, CHICKPEA, AND LENTIL TACOS ... 51

Crispy Chickpea Tacos with Vegan Caesar Dressing ... **52**
Mediterranean Chickpea Tacos ... **55**
BBQ Lentil Tacos ... **56**
Crispy Sheet Pan Tacos with Pinto Beans ... **59**
Sweet Potato and Black Bean Tostadas ... **60**
Crispy Baked Falafel Tacos ... **63**
Spicy Plantain and Black Bean Tacos ... **64**
Harissa Roasted Cauliflower and Chickpea Tacos ... **67**
Chimichurri Grilled Veggie and White Bean Tacos ... **68**
Pinto Bean and Avocado Corn Salsa Tostadas ... **71**
Smoky Lentil Tacos with Avocado ... **72**

CHAPTER 4
CAULIFLOWER, CORN, AND POTATO TACOS ... 75

Blackened Cauliflower Tacos with Chipotle Aioli ... **76**
Mexican-Style Street Corn Tacos ... **79**
Curried Potato and Cauliflower Tacos ... **80**
Roasted Corn and Poblano Tacos ... **83**

Buffalo Cauliflower Tacos with Jalapeño Ranch ... **84**
Spicy Potato Tacos ... **87**
Bang Bang Cauliflower Tacos ... **88**
Cauliflower Walnut Tacos ... **91**
Crispy BBQ Cauliflower Tacos ... **92**
Spicy Peanut Sweet Potato Tacos ... **95**
Sticky Sesame Ginger Cauliflower Tacos ... **96**

CHAPTER 5

PLANT-POWERED PROTEIN TACOS ... 99

Baja Tofu Tacos with Citrus Crema ... **100**
Grilled Tofu and Pineapple Taco ... **103**
Teriyaki Tempeh Tacos with Pineapple Salsa ... **106**
Sheet Pan Tofu and Fajita Veggie Tacos ... **109**
Butternut Squash and Soy Chorizo Tacos ... **110**
Korean-Style Tofu Tacos ... **113**
Soy Chorizo Tacos with Mango Salsa ... **114**
Greek Gyro-Style Tempeh Tacos ... **117**
Tofu Carnitas Tacos with Apple Salsa ... **118**
Coconut-Crusted Tofu Tacos ... **121**
Maple Miso Tempeh Tacos ... **122**

CHAPTER 6

VEGGIE LOADED TACOS ... 125

Miso-Glazed Mushroom Tacos ... **126**
Jerk Plantain Tacos with Mango Salsa ... **129**
Crispy Avocado Tacos ... **130**
BBQ Jackfruit Tacos ... **133**
Delicata Squash Tacos with Maple Tahini ... **134**
Smoky Butternut Squash and Apple Tacos ... **137**
Mushroom Bánh Mì–Style Tacos ... **138**
Jackfruit Carnitas Tostadas ... **141**
Roasted Portobello Mushroom Tacos ... **142**
Gochujang Sweet Potato Street Tacos ... **145**
Chipotle Roasted Brussels Sprout Tacos ... **146**

ACKNOWLEDGMENTS ... 149
ABOUT THE AUTHOR ... 150
INDEX ... 153

INTRODUCTION:
MAKING TACO TUESDAY VEGAN

It's Tuesday night and I am tired from a full day of work, fighting traffic, and rushing to daycare pickup. I haven't given dinner a single thought. Do we even have groceries? My toddler is pulling at my pant leg. I'm buying time by offering her snacks against my better judgment; doing so will spoil her appetite for the meal I'm eventually going to make. To say I am short on time, energy, and patience is an understatement. I'm also hungry.

This is what a typical weeknight used to look like for me and my family. To be honest, it's still a struggle sometimes. I'm just not someone who plans a full weekly menu, spends hours meal prepping, and has every last dinner detail nailed down to the garnish. Plus, I like to keep some flexibility in our schedule to accommodate cravings, requests, and those really exhausting days when we just want to order takeout.

While I don't have my entire week of meals planned on Sunday night, I do find it helpful to follow a formula that eliminates at least one variable from the question, "What's for dinner?" As it turns out, I'm not the only one in need of some mealtime structure. As a millennial mom, I'm following no less than 100 parenting accounts on Instagram, and one of them is Kate Strickler from the blog *Naptime Kitchen*. Kate implemented "Pasta Monday" when her daughter was

a newborn as a way to have one less decision to make at the end of a long, hard day. While some may find this weekly ritual boring and repetitive, I was inspired by how a little bit of structure can inspire fun and creativity in the kitchen.

I've been using "Taco Tuesday" as a way to remove stress from dinnertime one night a week ever since my daughter, June, could chew. My go-to, zero-effort meal for her has always been a quesadilla. It's quick and easy to make, and I know she will happily eat it. When I found myself regularly sneaking bites from June's dinner plate, I decided to make Taco Tuesday something the whole family could enjoy. Keeping a stocked pantry and spice rack means I always have something on hand to whip up delicious plant-based tacos. When I remember to plan ahead, we explore new ingredients, flavors, and textures. As an added bonus, we've found that Taco Tuesday encourages our picky toddler to try new foods within the familiarity of a tortilla.

THE ESSENTIALS

My kitchen is tiny and I don't have a pantry so I'm very particular about the grocery items I keep on hand. Luckily, the essentials for a successful Taco Tuesday don't take up much space, and they have a long shelf life so you can stock up when they're on sale. These are the oil, spices, sweeteners, tortillas, and beans I recommend keeping in your kitchen so you're always prepared to make delicious plant-based tacos.

OIL AND SPICES

Avocado oil is my go-to cooking oil for Taco Tuesday and every other night of the week. Don't get me wrong; I love olive oil in a salad dressing where I want the flavor of the oil to shine through. But I have found that avocado oil is more versatile for cooking. It has a very mild flavor and a higher smoke point than olive oil, up to 500°F (250°C). If you have an avocado allergy or can't source avocado oil from your local supermarket, feel free to swap it for extra-virgin olive oil in any recipe.

I always have a few packets of **taco seasoning** in my spice drawer for convenience. I have made my own taco seasonings in the past, and I personally don't find the extra time and effort to offer better flavor. I really like the Siete brand of taco seasoning because it's made with simple ingredients and is free of preservatives, dairy, and grains. If you prefer the do-it-yourself method, making a large batch of taco seasoning is a great way to save time on busy weeknights.

Here's a list of other spices to have on hand:

Chili powder

Garlic powder

Onion powder

Cumin

Oregano

Paprika

Smoked paprika

Chipotle chili powder

Fine sea salt

Finally, I recommend having a black pepper grinder. The depth of flavor that freshly cracked black pepper offers over pre-ground black pepper is substantial.

SWEETENERS

As for sweeteners, my favorites are **agave nectar** and **maple syrup**. Agave has a neutral flavor that is slightly sweeter than sugar while maple syrup has a distinct, full-bodied taste. Despite having a stronger flavor profile, pure maple syrup is my preferred sweetener for sweetening sauces and marinades. Agave nectar is generally sweeter than maple syrup, so if you choose to use agave nectar as a substitute, you may want to use slightly less than the recipe calls for and adjust from there.

TORTILLAS

You'll notice that all of the recipes in this book are photographed in **tortillas**. These are tacos, after all. I have tested each of these recipes on corn and flour tortillas, and my preferred type is noted in the ingredient list. If you have a strong preference or dietary restriction, use whichever tortilla you like best. I only have one request: Warm your tortillas! It makes such a big difference in the overall taste and mouthfeel of eating a taco. My favorite way is to carefully toast each tortilla over an open flame on my stovetop. You can also wrap a stack of tortillas in aluminum foil and bake them in the oven at 350°F (180°C, or gas mark 4) for 15 to 20 minutes. Unless otherwise noted in a recipe, opt for taco-size tortillas that are roughly 6 inches (15 cm) in diameter.

BEANS

Beans are the backbone of many of the plant-based tacos in this book. I chose to use canned beans for the convenience of whipping up a quick meal. When possible, use low-sodium beans; you can always add salt in the cooking process. If you prefer to use dried beans, ¾ cup (4¾ oz) of dried beans is equivalent to roughly one 15-ounce (425 g) can of beans. You'll need to soak dried beans overnight and then cook them on the stove or in a pressure cooker until tender. **Pinto beans**, **black beans**, **cannellini beans**, and **chickpeas** are great staples to have on-hand.

OTHER PANTRY ITEMS

Here's a list of the other pantry items you'll find convenient to have stocked for Taco Tuesday:

Canned chipotle peppers in adobo sauce

Canned green chiles (mild)

Vegan mayo

Nutritional yeast

Vegetable broth

Low-sodium soy sauce

Tamari

Toasted sesame oil

Rice vinegar

White vinegar

Vegan BBQ sauce

SERVING SIZES AND PORTIONS

I have found that two to three tacos is a satisfying serving size for most of the recipes in this book. Of course, the number of people a recipe will serve depends on if you're feeding little kids, hungry teens, or adults, as well as whether you are serving the tacos with a salad or side dish. The number of tortillas in the ingredient list indicates how many tacos a recipe will yield. With this knowledge in mind, feel free to scale a recipe up or down to accommodate your Taco Tuesday dinner guests.

> **CHAPTER 1** <

THE BASICS: TORTILLAS, SALSAS, AND SAUCES

When tacos are in regular rotation on your dinner menu, having a handful of basic recipes in your back pocket will serve you well. It may not be realistic for you to make homemade Flour Tortillas (page 19) or Corn Tortillas (page 16) every Tuesday. It certainly isn't for me! But on those occasions when you do have an extra 20 minutes, making tortillas is a fun and rewarding way to craft your Taco Tuesday meal completely from scratch.

I can't overstate how worthwhile it is to make your own salsa. Much of the process is hands-off, and salsa stays fresh in the fridge for up to a week. Salsa will also keep in the freezer for up to four months, making it a great weekend meal prep activity. Flavorful sauces like Jalapeño Ranch (page 30) and Chipotle Aioli (page 26) can even go beyond the taco and spice up your meals any night of the week.

CORN TORTILLAS

MAKES 8 TORTILLAS   To make corn tortillas you need a bag of masa harina, which is nixtamalized (processed) ground corn. Regular cornmeal won't do! You can find masa harina in the same aisle as beans, tortillas, and salsas at the grocery store.

1 cup (116 g) white or yellow masa harina
½ teaspoon fine sea salt
¾ cup (175 ml) warm water

1. In a large bowl, whisk together the masa harina and salt.

2. Pour the warm water into the bowl and use a spoon or your hands to mix the water into the dry ingredients, until a ball of dough begins to form.

3. Knead the dough for 2 to 3 minutes to hydrate the masa harina. The dough should feel springy, firm, and moist. If the dough is sticking to your hands, add a touch more masa harina. If the dough feels dry, add a teaspoon of water.

4. Soak a kitchen towel and wring out the water. Place the damp towel over the ball of dough and let it rest for 10 minutes.

5. Meanwhile, heat a cast iron skillet over medium-high heat. Prepare 2 circular pieces of plastic wrap or parchment paper the size of your tortilla press.

6. Split the dough into 8 equal pieces and roll them into balls about the size of a golf ball. Set them on a cutting board or countertop and cover with the damp towel.

7. Place a piece of plastic wrap or parchment paper on the bottom plate of a tortilla press. Set the first ball of dough in the center of the plate and place the other piece of plastic wrap or parchment paper on top of the dough.

8. Press down with the tortilla press to flatten the dough as much as possible. It should be about 1⁄16-inch (2 mm) thick. Carefully peel the flattened dough off of the plastic wrap or parchment paper and place it in the hot pan.

9. Cook for 1 minute on the first side, then flip the tortilla. If it looks dry, spray it with water. Cook for another minute on the second side, until a few dark spots appear on the surface of the tortilla. Flip once more and cook on the other side, until the tortilla puffs up slightly.

10. Transfer the tortilla to a plate and cover with a warm towel or place in a tortilla warmer. Repeat with the remaining balls of dough.

11. These corn tortillas are best enjoyed fresh. You can also make them ahead of time and store them in the refrigerator in an airtight container for up to 2 days. To reheat, warm the tortillas on the stove in a skillet with a spritz of water to keep them soft.

TOSTADA SHELLS

2 tablespoons (30 ml) avocado oil
1 tablespoon (15 ml) lime juice
8 corn tortillas

1. Preheat the oven to 350°F (180°C, or gas mark 4) and line a large baking sheet or 2 smaller baking sheets with parchment paper.

2. Combine the avocado oil and lime juice in a small bowl. Arrange the corn tortillas in a single layer on the baking sheet(s). Lightly brush both sides of each tortilla with the lime juice and avocado oil mixture.

3. Bake the tortillas for 8 minutes, then use tongs to flip the tortillas and bake for 8 minutes more. When done, they should be golden and crisp. Transfer the tostada shells to a wire rack to cool.

HARD TACO SHELLS

8 corn tortillas
Avocado oil cooking spray

1. Place a piece of aluminum foil on the bottom rack of the oven. Preheat the oven to 400°F (200°C, or gas mark 6).

2. Working two at a time, wrap your corn tortillas in a damp paper towel and microwave for 30 seconds. The paper towel and tortillas will be very hot; use caution when removing the tortillas from the microwave.

3. Carefully coat both sides of each tortilla with avocado oil cooking spray.

4. Using tongs to protect your hands, drape a tortilla over 2 oven grates on the top rack of the oven. Gently press down on the left and right sides of the tortilla so they hang below the grates. Repeat with the remaining tortillas.

5. Bake the taco shells for 8 minutes, until golden and crisp.

6. Use tongs to gently release the taco shells from the oven grate. The taco shells should be in the shape of a big letter *U* with a flat bottom.

FLOUR TORTILLAS

MAKES 8 TORTILLAS If you have the time, making flour tortillas from scratch is incredibly rewarding. It takes a lot of practice to master a perfectly round flour tortilla, so don't stress if the shape isn't perfect.

1½ cups (188 g) all-purpose flour
½ teaspoon baking powder
½ teaspoon fine sea salt
½ cup (120 ml) warm water
¼ cup (60 ml) avocado oil

1. In a large bowl, whisk together the all-purpose flour, baking powder, and salt.

2. In a smaller bowl, combine the warm water and avocado oil.

3. Pour the wet ingredients into the dry ingredients. Stir with a large spoon to combine.

4. When the dough becomes too thick to stir, use your hands to knead the dough into a smooth ball. If the dough feels wet and sticky, add a touch more flour.

5. Set the dough in the bowl and cover with a clean kitchen towel. Let it rest for 10 minutes.

6. Heat a nonstick skillet over medium heat. Divide the dough into 8 equal balls about the size of a golf ball.

7. Roll the first ball of dough between your hands and place it down on a floured surface. Press down on the ball of dough with your palm to flatten it into a circle.

8. Sprinkle a bit of flour on top of the dough and use a rolling pin to roll and flatten the circle as thin as possible, about 1/16 inch (2 mm).

9. Carefully pick up the flattened dough and place it in the hot pan. Cook for 1 minute, then flip and cook for 1 minute on the other side. Transfer the finished tortilla to a plate and cover with a warm towel.

10. Repeat the process with the remaining balls of dough. These flour tortillas are best enjoyed fresh, but will keep in a sealed bag for 2 days at room temperature and for up to 5 days in the refrigerator.

THE BASICS: TORTILLAS, SALSAS, AND SAUCES

GUACAMOLE

MAKES 2 CUPS (450 G)   Every taco lover needs a solid guacamole recipe in their back pocket. This one uses all fresh ingredients and is a perfect base for experimenting. Try adding finely chopped jalapeño or tomato to make it your own.

4 ripe avocados
2 tablespoons (30 ml) lime juice
1 teaspoon fresh garlic, grated
¼ cup (4 g) finely chopped fresh cilantro
3 tablespoons (30 g) finely chopped red onion
½ teaspoon fine sea salt

1. Slice the avocados in half lengthwise and discard the pits. Squeeze the avocado flesh into a medium bowl. Use a fork to mash the avocado to your desired texture.

2. Add the lime juice, garlic, cilantro, red onion, and salt. Mix to combine the ingredients with the mashed avocado.

3. Serve the guacamole immediately for the best flavor and texture or store in an airtight container in the refrigerator for up to 3 days.

SALSA VERDE

MAKES 2 CUPS (512 G)   I love having a jar of home-made salsa verde in my fridge at all times because it amplifies the flavor of so many of my favorite foods. This recipe can lean spicy depending on how hot your jalapeño is, so use half or skip it all together for a mild salsa verde.

1½ pounds (680 g) tomatillos, peeled and rinsed
   (about 12 small tomatillos)
1 jalapeño pepper
2 poblano peppers
1 tablespoon (15 ml) avocado oil
¼ cup (40 g) chopped white onion
1 garlic clove
½ cup (8 g) fresh cilantro leaves
3 tablespoons (45 ml) lime juice, plus more as needed
½ teaspoon fine sea salt, plus more as needed
½ teaspoon agave
1 ripe avocado, peeled and diced (optional)

1. Preheat the oven to 425°F (220°C, or gas mark 7) and line a baking sheet with aluminum foil.

2. Place the tomatillos, jalapeño, and poblano peppers on the foil and drizzle with avocado oil. Toss to coat.

3. Roast the tomatillos and peppers for 20 minutes, then flip and roast for 10 minutes more. When done, everything should be nicely charred and tender. Remove the baking sheet from the oven and allow the vegetables to cool slightly.

4. Slice the stems off the poblano peppers and jalapeño. Cut the jalapeño in half, scoop out the seeds, and discard them.

5. Transfer the roasted tomatillos and peppers to a food processor. Add the onion, garlic, cilantro, lime juice, salt, and agave.

6. Run the food processor until the peppers and tomatillos break down and combine with the rest of the ingredients. Add a splash of water if the salsa seems too thick. Taste and add more salt or lime juice to brighten the flavor, if desired.

7. To make a creamy salsa verde, add a diced avocado to the food processor and run until fully blended. Enjoy immediately or transfer to a container with a tight-fitting lid and store in the fridge for up to a week.

SALSA ROJA

MAKES 4 CUPS (908 G)   The ancho chile is one of the most popular chiles in Mexican cuisine. It gives a sweet, smoky flavor to this salsa roja recipe and thickens it up perfectly. You can find dried ancho chiles with other dried Mexican chili peppers and spices at most larger grocery stores.

1 dried ancho chile
2 pounds (910 g) Roma tomatoes
1 white onion, peeled and quartered
1 jalapeño, halved and seeds removed
1½ tablespoons (25 ml) avocado oil
⅓ cup (5 g) packed fresh cilantro leaves
2 garlic cloves
3 tablespoons (45 ml) lime juice
2 teaspoons fine sea salt

1. Place the dried ancho chile in a bowl and cover it with hot water. Set something slightly heavy, like a mug or smaller bowl, on top of the chile so it stays submerged in the water. Set it aside to soak.

2. Preheat the oven to 450°F (230°C, or gas mark 8) and line a large baking sheet with aluminum foil.

3. Place the tomatoes, onion, and jalapeño on the baking sheet and drizzle with avocado oil. Roast the vegetables for 20 minutes, flipping halfway through, until tender and caramelized. Remove the baking sheet from the oven and allow the vegetables to cool slightly.

4. Slice open the ancho chile and remove the stem and seeds. Tear the chile into pieces.

5. Transfer the vegetables to a blender or food processor. Add the ancho chile, cilantro, garlic, lime juice, and salt. Blend until smooth, adding a touch of water if the salsa is too thick. Adjust the salt to taste.

6. Allow the salsa to cool to room temperature before transferring it to a jar. This salsa roja will last up to a week in the refrigerator and as long as 3 months in the freezer.

CASHEW QUESO

2 CUPS (448 G)   I have fooled so many non-vegan friends with this cashew queso. It's so impossibly creamy and "cheesy" without containing any processed vegan cheese. Use this recipe in place of vegan cheese in any recipe with delicious results.

1 cup (110 g) diced golden potatoes
¼ cup (33 g) diced carrot
⅓ cup (55 g) diced yellow onion
1 cup (235 ml) water
¼ cup (32 g) raw cashews
⅓ cup (75 g) vegan butter
1 teaspoon fine sea salt
1 garlic clove
¼ teaspoon Dijon mustard
1 tablespoon (15 ml) lemon juice
¼ teaspoon paprika
½ teaspoon chili powder
½ package (12 ounces, or 240 g) soy chorizo

1. Combine the potatoes, carrot, onion, water, and cashews in a saucepan and bring to a boil over medium heat. Cover and simmer until the vegetables are soft, about 15 minutes.

2. Pour the entire contents of the saucepan into a high speed blender. Add the vegan butter, salt, garlic, Dijon mustard, lemon juice, paprika, and chili powder. Blend until smooth and creamy.

3. In a nonstick skillet, cook the soy chorizo over medium-high heat for 5 minutes, stirring occasionally. Pour the cashew queso into the skillet and stir to incorporate the soy chorizo. Turn off the heat and serve or store in a covered container in the refrigerator for up to 5 days.

CHIPOTLE AIOLI

1 CUP (225 G) This chipotle aioli couldn't be easier to make, and it's best when made fresh. Transfer the remaining chipotle peppers in adobo sauce to an airtight container and store in the refrigerator for up to four days for use in another recipe.

1 cup (225 g) vegan mayo
¼ teaspoon garlic powder
⅛ teaspoon fine sea salt
3 chipotle peppers from a can of chipotle peppers in adobo sauce
1 teaspoon maple syrup

1. Scoop the vegan mayo into a small blender or food processor. Add the garlic powder, salt, chipotle peppers, and maple syrup.

2. Blend until smooth, adding a teaspoon of water if needed to thin. The chipotle aioli can be stored in an airtight container in the refrigerator for up to 1 week.

PICKLED RED ONION

1 CUP (235 ML) I always have a jar of pickled red onion in my refrigerator. It comes together quickly and stays fresh in the fridge for 2 to 3 weeks.

½ cup (120 ml) white vinegar
½ cup (120 ml) filtered water
1 teaspoon sugar
½ teaspoon fine sea salt
½ large red onion, thinly sliced

1. Pour the vinegar and water into a small saucepan and set the heat to medium-low. When the liquid is hot, add the sugar and salt and stir until dissolved. Turn off the heat.

2. Add the red onion slices to a 16-ounce (475 ml) jar or a similarly sized glass container with a lid. When the pickling liquid has cooled a bit, pour it over the onions. Press down on the onions with the back of a spoon to submerge them in the pickling liquid.

3. Allow the onions to sit at room temperature until the liquid has completely cooled, then twist the lid on tightly. Store the pickled red onion in the refrigerator for up to 3 weeks.

MANGO SALSA

4 CUPS (1 KG) Mango salsa tastes good on nearly any taco. If you happen upon a perfectly ripe mango at the grocery store, snatch it up and make a batch of this mango salsa for Taco Tuesday this week.

2 mangoes, peeled and finely diced
1 red bell pepper, finely diced
1 jalapeño, finely diced
½ cup (8 g) finely chopped fresh cilantro
⅓ cup (55 g) finely diced red onion
1 tablespoon (15 ml) lime juice
½ teaspoon fine sea salt

1. Add all of the ingredients to a medium mixing bowl and toss to combine. Store leftovers in a tightly sealed container in the refrigerator for up to 3 days.

JALAPEÑO RANCH

2½ CUPS (570 ML)   This is the taco sauce of my dreams. It's creamy, thanks to avocado and cashews, spicy, and fresh. Drizzle this Jalapeño Ranch on any taco to add zippy flavor.

2 avocados
¼ cup (32 g) chopped raw cashews
1 jalapeño, seeds removed and chopped
1 garlic clove
½ cup (8 g) fresh cilantro leaves
¼ cup (60 ml) lime juice
1 teaspoon fine sea salt
1¼ cups (285 ml) filtered water

1. Slice the avocados in half lengthwise and discard the pits. Squeeze the avocado flesh into a blender. Add the cashews, jalapeño, garlic, cilantro, lime juice, salt, and water.

2. Blend until completely smooth. This might take a few minutes if you don't have a powerful blender. If the sauce is too thick, add another splash of water and blend until pourable. It can be stored in an airtight container in the refrigerator for up to 3 days.

> ❯ **CHAPTER 2** ❮

VEGAN CHEESY TACOS

It's amazing how far vegan cheese has come over the last fifteen years. What used to be something I avoided at all costs now makes a regular appearance on my grocery list. If you have been dairy-free for any length of time, you've probably dabbled in the vegan cheese arena and know what you like (and what you don't like). Personally, I prefer sliced vegan cheese over shredded. I think the taste is superior, and it melts wonderfully. Take some liberties with the recipes in this chapter and use the vegan cheeses you know and love.

Of course, you may be someone who does not like the taste or texture of vegan cheese. That is totally fair! If you prefer to make your own vegan cheese, my Cashew Queso (page 24) can be spread on a tortilla or drizzled over a taco for a delicious "cheesy" flavor. Whatever you do, don't skip the Cheesy Smashburger Tacos (page 37). They're so savory and satisfying and will please even the pickiest eaters at your dinner table.

CRISPY BLACK BEAN AND CASHEW QUESO TACOS

SERVES 4 TO 6 These are the tacos I make on chilly nights when I don't mind turning on the oven. The crispy taco shells and "cheesy" filling offer such a satisfying combination! They require minimal effort and the payoff is huge. I love making sheet pan tacos for the convenience and ease of prep and serving. Plus, cleanup is a breeze. You can serve these tacos right off the sheet pan or transfer them to a serving platter. Everyone in my family adores these Crispy Black Bean and Cashew Queso Tacos.

2½ cups (560 g) Cashew Queso (page 24)
1 can (15 ounces, or 425 g) low-sodium black beans, drained and rinsed
12 flour tortillas
Avocado oil cooking spray

TO SERVE
Vegan sour cream
Pico de gallo
Lime wedges

1. Combine the cashew queso and the black beans in a large skillet and set over medium-low heat. Cook for 5 to 10 minutes, stirring occasionally, until heated through.

2. Just before filling, warm your tortillas by wrapping them in a damp paper towel and microwaving for 15 seconds. Alternatively, you can heat them one at a time in a dry skillet over medium heat for 30 seconds on each side. This will prevent the tortillas from cracking when you fold them in half.

3. Preheat the oven to 400°F (200°C, or gas mark 6) and line a large baking sheet or 2 smaller baking sheets with parchment paper.

4. Working one at a time, spray both sides of each tortilla with avocado oil cooking spray.

5. Spoon a few tablespoons (45 ml) of the veggie and bean mixture into the middle of each tortilla, then fold in half and place in a single layer on the prepared baking sheet. Repeat with all of the tortillas and remaining taco filling.

6. Bake the tacos for 20 minutes. When done, they should look golden and crispy.

7. To serve, top the crispy tacos with vegan sour cream and pico de gallo. Serve with lime wedges on the side.

CHEESY SMASHBURGER TACOS

SERVES 4   In this recipe, the TikTok smashburger taco trend goes plant-based. I dream about this taco! Seasoned Impossible Ground Beef gets smashed flat onto a tortilla in a hot pan, topped with melty vegan cheese, and finished off with shredded lettuce, pickles, and crispy fried onion. Don't skip the vegan burger sauce—it adds creamy texture and a delicious tangy zip.

1 package (12 ounces, or 340 g) Impossible Ground Beef
1 teaspoon smoked paprika
½ teaspoon onion powder
½ teaspoon garlic powder
½ teaspoon oregano
½ teaspoon fine sea salt
Freshly cracked black pepper
Avocado oil, for cooking
8 flour tortillas
8 slices vegan cheese

FOR THE VEGAN BURGER SAUCE
½ cup (115 g) vegan mayo
¼ cup (68 g) ketchup
1 tablespoon (15 g) sweet relish
1 teaspoon yellow mustard
¼ teaspoon garlic powder
¼ teaspoon onion powder
¼ teaspoon paprika
Pinch fine sea salt
¼ teaspoon white vinegar

TO SERVE
Shredded lettuce
Pickle chips
Crispy fried onion

1. Preheat the oven to 300°F (150°C , or gas mark 2).

2. Unwrap the Impossible Ground Beef and place in a large mixing bowl. Add the smoked paprika, onion powder, garlic powder, oregano, salt, and pepper. Use a gloved hand to thoroughly mix the seasonings into the Impossible Ground Beef.

3. On a large plate, roll the vegan burger mixture into 8 pieces of equal size, a little bigger than a golf ball. Set aside.

4. To make the vegan burger sauce: Combine all of the ingredients in a medium bowl and mix well to combine. Set aside.

5. Warm a teaspoon of avocado oil in a nonstick skillet over medium-high heat. When the oil is hot, place 1 portion of the vegan burger mixture in the skillet and set a tortilla on top of it.

6. Press down on the tortilla with a heavy measuring cup or coffee mug to smash the burger into a flat patty. Cook for 3 minutes, then use a spatula to flip the taco. The vegan burger should be stuck to the tortilla and browned and crisp on top.

7. Place a slice of vegan cheese on top of the vegan burger. Add a teaspoon of water to the skillet and cover it with a lid. Cook the cheesy smashburger taco covered for 2 minutes, until the vegan cheese has melted and the tortilla is crisp.

8. Transfer the cheesy smashburger taco to a large baking sheet. Keep the baking sheet in the warm oven while you make the remaining tacos, adding each taco to the baking sheet as you finish cooking them.

9. To serve, top each taco with vegan burger sauce, shredded lettuce, pickles, and crispy fried onion. Or set your favorite burger toppings out for everyone to make their own.

VEGAN CHEESY TACOS

CHILE RELLENO–STYLE TACOS

....

SERVES 4 Chile relleno is a Mexican dish in which a chile, usually an Anaheim or poblano pepper, is stuffed with cheese, battered, and fried until golden and crisp. This taco recipe is inspired by authentic chile relleno but is deconstructed and entirely plant-based. If you are sensitive to spicy foods, don't sweat it; poblano peppers are considered mild. They pack much less heat than a jalapeño but are a little spicier than a bell pepper.

4 poblano peppers
1 tablespoon (15 ml) avocado oil
1 package (12 ounces, or 340 g) Impossible Ground Beef
½ tablespoon chili powder
½ teaspoon cumin
½ teaspoon oregano
½ teaspoon fine sea salt
Freshly cracked black pepper
2 garlic cloves, grated
Avocado oil spray
8 corn tortillas
8 ounces (225 g) vegan cheese (Mexican-style, mozzarella, or pepper jack)

TO SERVE
Salsa Roja (page 23)
Fresh cilantro

1. Preheat the oven to 400°F (200°C, or gas mark 6) and line a baking sheet with aluminum foil.

2. Place the poblano peppers on the baking sheet and roast for 35 to 40 minutes, flipping halfway through. When done, the peppers should be blackened and tender.

3. Transfer the poblano peppers to a bowl and cover it with a plate to steam. Leave the oven on.

4. Meanwhile, make the filling. Warm the avocado oil in a large skillet over medium-high heat. Add the Impossible Ground Beef and break it up with a spatula. Season with chili powder, cumin, oregano, salt, and pepper.

5. Continue to cook and stir the Impossible Ground Beef mixture until browned, about 5 minutes. Add the grated garlic and cook the mixture for 1 minute more. Turn off the heat.

6. When the poblano peppers are cool enough to handle, remove the stems and peel the skins. It's okay if the softened peppers begin to pull apart into chunks. Hold the pepper pieces under running water to wash away the seeds, then transfer them to a plate. Pat dry with a paper towel.

7. Discard the aluminum foil used to roast the peppers and lightly coat the baking sheet with avocado oil spray.

8. Place 8 corn tortillas on the baking sheet in a single layer. It's okay if they overlap a little bit. Top each tortilla with a few pieces of poblano pepper. Divide the Impossible Ground Beef mixture between each taco and top each one with vegan cheese.

9. Bake the tacos for 5 to 7 minutes, until the vegan cheese has melted and the tortilla is slightly crisp.

10. To serve, garnish each taco with Salsa Roja and cilantro.

JALAPEÑO POPPER TAQUITOS

SERVES 4 Jalapeño poppers are one of my all-time favorite appetizers. Instead of stuffing jalapeños here, the peppers are chopped and folded into a creamy nondairy cream cheese mixture that offers the perfect blend of savory and spicy. Everything is wrapped up in corn tortillas and baked until crisp. Serve with chipotle ranch dressing and fresh cilantro for an easy and satisfying weeknight meal.

5 ounces (140 g) broccoli florets, finely chopped
   or shredded (about 1½ cups)
3 tablespoons (45 ml) water
1 package (8 ounces, or 225 g) plain nondairy
   cream cheese
1 container (5 ounces, or 140 g) plain, unsweetened
   nondairy yogurt
2 jalapeños, seeds removed and finely chopped
2 scallions, dark and light green parts finely chopped
½ teaspoon garlic powder
½ teaspoon fine sea salt
12 corn tortillas
12 slices vegan cheddar cheese
Avocado oil cooking spray

FOR THE CHIPOTLE RANCH
½ cup (120 ml) vegan ranch dressing
1½ teaspoons sauce from a can of chipotle peppers
   in adobo

TO SERVE
Fresh cilantro

1. Preheat the oven to 400°F (200°C, or gas mark 6) and line a baking sheet with aluminum foil.

2. Place a nonstick pan over medium heat. Transfer the broccoli to the pan and add 3 tablespoons (45 ml) of water. Cover the pan and steam the broccoli for 3 minutes, until bright green. Uncover the pan and set aside.

3. In a large bowl, combine the nondairy cream cheese, nondairy yogurt, jalapeños, scallions, garlic powder, and salt. Mix well to combine.

4. When the broccoli has cooled slightly, drain any water that is left over in the pan and pat the broccoli dry with a few paper towels. Mix the broccoli into the nondairy cream cheese mixture.

5. To make sure your tortillas don't crack when you roll them, you'll need to soften them in the microwave. Wrap 2 tortillas in damp paper towels and microwave for 30 seconds. Use a pair of tongs to remove the tortillas from the microwave—they'll be extremely hot.

6. Place a slice of vegan cheddar cheese in the center of the warm tortilla and top with a few tablespoons of the broccoli-jalapeño mixture. Roll up the taquito and place it seam-side down on the prepared baking sheet. Lightly coat the outside of the taquito with avocado oil spray.

7. Repeat this process with the remaining tortillas, vegan cheddar cheese, and filling, working 2 tortillas at a time to ensure they are warm and soft when rolling them up.

8. Line up the taquitos on the baking sheet spaced 1 inch (2.5 cm) apart. Bake them for 16 to 18 minutes, until golden and crisp.

9. To make the chipotle ranch: Mix together the vegan ranch dressing and adobo sauce in a small bowl.

10. To serve, drizzle the taquitos with chipotle ranch or serve the sauce on the side. Top with cilantro.

LOADED TATER TOT TACOS

....

SERVES 4 TO 5 Once you eat tater tots wrapped in a tortilla and topped with beans, corn, melty vegan cheese, and all of your favorite taco toppings—you'll never go back. Crispy tater tots are the perfect vehicle for all of the spicy, savory, and pickled flavors in this recipe. You can serve these tacos fully loaded with everything or offer the garnishes on the side so everyone at your table can build their own.

1 bag (32 ounces, or 910 g) frozen tater tots
2 teaspoons avocado oil
1 can (15 ounces, or 425 g) black beans, drained and rinsed
1 can (15 ounces, or 425 g) corn, drained
2 tablespoons (18 g) taco seasoning
10 flour tortillas
1 bag (7 ounces, or 200 g) shredded Mexican-style vegan cheese

TO SERVE
Pickled Red Onion (page 27)
Vegan sour cream
1 jalapeño, sliced
1 avocado, peeled and sliced
Fresh cilantro, chopped
Pico de gallo

1. Preheat the oven to 450°F (230°C, or gas mark 8) and line a baking sheet with parchment paper.

2. Arrange the tater tots in a single layer on the baking sheet and bake for 20 minutes, or until golden and crisp.

3. Meanwhile, warm the avocado oil in a pan over medium heat. When the oil is hot, add the black beans and corn. Sauté for 8 to 10 minutes, stirring occasionally, until the corn is golden and fragrant. Sprinkle the taco seasoning into the pan and sauté for 5 minutes more.

4. Remove the tater tots from the oven and lower the oven temperature to 350°F (180°C, or gas mark 4). Transfer the tater tots to a plate.

5. Arrange the tortillas on the baking sheet in a single layer (it's okay if they overlap a little bit). Place a few tater tots on each tortilla and top with the bean and corn mixture. Sprinkle some vegan cheese over each taco.

6. Return the baking sheet to the oven and bake the tacos for 10 minutes, until the vegan cheese has melted.

7. To serve, top each taco with Pickled Red Onion, vegan sour cream, jalapeño, avocado, cilantro, and pico de gallo. Or offer toppings on the side for everyone to create their own perfect taco.

CHEESY POTATO TACOS

SERVES 4   There's no better duo than potatoes and cheese. In this taco, Yukon gold potatoes are roasted until crisp on the outside and fluffy on the inside. Be sure not to crowd the potatoes on the baking sheet or they will get soft instead of crispy. Stuffed in a corn tortilla with melty vegan cheddar cheese and topped with cool vegan sour cream, pico de gallo, and cilantro, this recipe is a total crowd pleaser.

2 pounds (910 g) Yukon gold potatoes, diced into ½-inch (1.3 cm) cubes
2 tablespoons (30 ml) avocado oil
½ teaspoon onion powder
½ teaspoon garlic powder
1 teaspoon paprika
1 teaspoon fine sea salt
8 corn tortillas
8 slices vegan cheddar cheese

TO SERVE
Vegan sour cream
Pico de gallo
Fresh cilantro, chopped

1. Preheat the oven to 425°F (220°C, or gas mark 7) and line 2 baking sheets with parchment paper.

2. In a large mixing bowl, combine the potatoes, avocado oil, onion powder, garlic powder, paprika, and salt. Set a large plate or cutting board on top of the bowl and shake it to coat the potatoes.

3. Divide the potatoes between the baking sheets. Do not crowd the potatoes or they won't crisp up! Roast the potatoes for 20 minutes. Stir the potatoes and roast for 8 to 10 minutes more, until golden and crispy. Remove the baking sheets from the oven.

4. Lift up on the parchment paper on one of the baking sheets and transfer the potatoes to the other baking sheet.

5. Arrange the tortillas in a single layer on the empty baking sheet (be careful, it will be hot). Divide the crispy potatoes between the tortillas and top each with a slice of vegan cheese.

6. Return the baking sheet to the oven for 5 minutes, until the vegan cheese has melted.

7. To serve, top each taco with vegan sour cream, pico de gallo, and cilantro.

CHEESY AND CRUNCHY VEGAN GORDITAS

MAKES 4   In Mexican cuisine, a gordita is a thick tortilla with a pocket in the middle that is stuffed with cheese, meat, and veggies. In this recipe, inspired by the authentic version, we are using pita bread as a shortcut. A layer of melty vegan cheese binds the warm pita bread to a hard taco shell filled with seasoned Impossible Ground Beef, lettuce, tomato, and vegan sour cream. It's soft, crunchy, and super satisfying.

1 tablespoon (15 ml) avocado oil
1 package (12 ounces, or 340 g) Impossible Ground Beef
2½ tablespoons (23 g) taco seasoning
¾ cup (175 ml) vegetable broth
4 pieces pita bread

TO SERVE
8 slices vegan cheddar cheese
¼ cup (60 ml) water, divided
4 Hard Taco Shells (page 18)
1 cup (47 g) shredded lettuce
2 Roma tomatoes, diced
Vegan sour cream

1. Warm the avocado oil in a large skillet over medium heat. When the oil is hot, add the Impossible Ground Beef and use a spatula to break it up into small pieces.

2. Sprinkle the taco seasoning over the Impossible Ground Beef and continue to cook for 5 to 7 minutes, stirring occasionally, until nicely browned.

3. Pour the vegetable broth into the skillet and turn the heat to low. Gently simmer for 10 minutes, until most of the liquid has cooked off and the "meat" is tender and juicy. Cover the skillet to keep warm.

4. Place a piece of pita bread in a small skillet over medium heat. Arrange 2 slices of vegan cheddar cheese side by side on top of the pita bread. Add 1 tablespoon (15 ml) of water to the pan and cover with a lid for about 2 minutes, until the vegan cheese has melted.

5. Meanwhile, fill a hard taco shell with Impossible Ground Beef and top with shredded lettuce, diced tomato, and vegan sour cream.

6. To serve, transfer the warm, cheesy pita bread to a plate. Place the hard taco shell in the center of the pita bread and fold up the sides. Repeat with the remaining ingredients to make 4 cheesy and crunchy vegan gorditas.

CHEESY BEAN AND RICE TAQUITOS

SERVES 4 Taquitos are a Mexican dish traditionally made with corn tortillas, but they can also be made with flour. This recipe uses flour tortillas—they're flexible and easy to roll up. For a corn tortilla taquito recipe, I highly recommend making my Jalapeño Popper Taquitos (page 41). Here, rice, pinto beans, bell pepper, and vegan cheddar cheese are rolled up in flour tortillas, baked until crispy, and served with homemade Salsa Roja for drizzling or dipping.

1 teaspoon avocado oil

3 garlic cloves, grated

1 red bell pepper, finely chopped

1 can (15 ounces, or 425 g) pinto beans, drained and rinsed

1½ tablespoons (14 g) taco seasoning

1 teaspoon sauce from a can of chipotle peppers in adobo sauce

8 slices vegan cheddar cheese

8 flour tortillas

2 cups (372 g) cooked white rice

Avocado oil spray

TO SERVE

Salsa Roja (page 23)

Vegan sour cream

Fresh cilantro

1. Preheat the oven to 375°F (190°C, or gas mark 5) and line a large baking sheet with parchment paper.

2. Warm the avocado oil in a nonstick pan over medium heat. When the oil is hot, add the garlic and sauté until fragrant, about 1 minute.

3. Add the red bell pepper to the saucepan and sauté, stirring occasionally, until the bell pepper has softened, about 5 minutes more.

4. Pour the pinto beans into the saucepan and sprinkle with taco seasoning. Add the adobo sauce and stir. Turn off the heat.

5. Place a slice of vegan cheese in the center of the first tortilla. Add a spoonful of rice down the center and top with a spoonful of the bean mixture. Roll up the tortilla and place it seam-side down on the prepared baking sheet. Repeat with the remaining vegan cheese, tortillas, rice, and beans.

6. Lightly coat the rolled up tortillas with avocado oil spray and bake in the hot oven for 10 minutes, until light golden and crisp.

7. To serve, drizzle Salsa Roja and vegan sour cream on top of the taquitos with fresh cilantro or serve alongside.

› **CHAPTER 3** ‹

BEAN, CHICKPEA, AND LENTIL TACOS

Legumes like beans, chickpeas, and lentils are versatile and hearty, making them fantastic taco fillings. In this chapter, you'll discover new ways to prepare and enjoy a variety of beans and lentils that will keep dinnertime exciting. Crispy Baked Falafel Tacos (page 63) will test your kitchen skills with homemade falafel (it's easy, I promise). If time is short, whip up dinner in minutes by making Pinto Bean and Avocado Corn Salsa Tostadas (page 71). This collection of recipes is packed with protein, fiber, and flavor.

If you don't regularly eat a lot of beans or lentils, you may have a difficult time digesting large quantities of legumes at first. I recommend starting with BBQ Lentil Tacos (page 56) or Smoky Lentil Tacos with Avocado (page 72). Lentils are tiny and generally considered easier to digest than larger beans. I hope this chapter broadens your horizons into cooking with beans and lentils and gives you some new tools for incorporating them into your diet.

CRISPY CHICKPEA TACOS WITH VEGAN CAESAR DRESSING

SERVES 4 My favorite way to make ultra-crispy chickpeas is in the air fryer. If you don't have an air fryer, you can roast your chickpeas on a baking sheet at 425°F (220°C, or gas mark 7) for 20 to 30 minutes, until they're golden brown and crisp. They lend fantastic texture and flavor to this salad-inspired taco complete with a creamy vegan Caesar dressing, shredded lettuce, avocado slices, and vegan parmesan cheese.

2 cans (14 ounces, or 395 g each) chickpeas, drained and rinsed
1 tablespoon (15 ml) avocado oil
½ teaspoon fine sea salt
½ teaspoon garlic powder
¼ teaspoon smoked paprika
Freshly cracked black pepper

FOR THE VEGAN CAESAR DRESSING
1 container (8 ounces, or 225 g) hummus (about 1 cup)
3 tablespoons (45 ml) lemon juice
2 teaspoons caper brine
1 teaspoon capers
½ teaspoon Dijon mustard
½ teaspoon maple syrup
2 garlic cloves, minced
¼ teaspoon fine sea salt
½ tablespoon nutritional yeast (optional)
3 tablespoons (45 ml) filtered water, to thin

TO SERVE
2 romaine hearts, finely chopped or shredded
8 flour tortillas, warmed
1 avocado, peeled and sliced
Vegan parmesan cheese (optional)

1. Line a large baking sheet with a clean kitchen towel. Dump the rinsed chickpeas onto the towel and shake the baking sheet back and forth to dry the chickpeas as much as possible.

2. Transfer the dried chickpeas to a bowl and drizzle with the avocado oil. Sprinkle with salt and gently stir to coat.

3. Transfer the chickpeas to the basket of an air fryer. Make sure the chickpeas are in a single layer and work in batches if necessary—this will ensure they get evenly crispy.

4. Cook the chickpeas at 390°F (200°C) for 10 minutes, shaking the basket halfway through. Be careful—the chickpeas may pop when exposed to the cool air in your kitchen. Shake the basket away from you just to be safe.

5. When the chickpeas are done, return them to the bowl and toss them with the garlic powder, smoked paprika, and pepper while they're still warm.

6. To make the vegan Caesar dressing: Combine all of the ingredients in a food processor or a small blender and blend until creamy and smooth. If you don't like nutritional yeast, the dressing still tastes great without it.

7. To serve, divide the shredded romaine between the tortillas and top with crispy chickpeas and avocado slices. Drizzle the vegan Caesar over the tacos or serve it in a small pitcher for everyone to dress their own. Sprinkle the tacos with vegan parmesan, if desired.

MEDITERRANEAN CHICKPEA TACOS

SERVES 4   One of my favorite cookbooks has a chickpea salad full of fresh veggies and herbs that I love taking as a cold side to potlucks and picnics. This recipe is inspired by that chickpea salad, but I added an irresistible vegan tzatziki to drizzle on top and folded it into a tortilla. Enjoy it as a sit-down meal for dinner or pack the chickpeas and veggies as a salad and bring your tortillas and sauce on the side for a delicious on-the-go lunch wherever your day takes you.

2 cans (15.5 ounces, or 440 g each) chickpeas, drained and rinsed
3 tablespoons (45 ml) extra-virgin olive oil
¼ cup (60 ml) lemon juice
¾ teaspoon fine sea salt
Freshly cracked black pepper
½ cup (30 g) finely chopped fresh parsley

FOR THE VEGAN TZATZIKI
1 cup (227 g) plain nondairy yogurt
1 tablespoon (4 g) finely chopped fresh dill
1 seedless cucumber, finely grated
1 small garlic clove, grated
2 teaspoons red wine vinegar
1 tablespoon (15 ml) lemon juice
½ teaspoon fine sea salt

TO SERVE
8 fajita-size tortillas, warmed
1 pint (284 g) cherry tomatoes, halved
2 Persian cucumber, sliced and quartered
1 cup (90 g) vegan feta

1. Combine the chickpeas, olive oil, lemon juice, salt, pepper, and fresh parsley in a mixing bowl and toss to combine. Refrigerate until ready to serve.

2. To make the vegan tzatziki: In another bowl, mix together the plain nondairy yogurt, dill, grated cucumber and garlic, vinegar, lemon juice, and salt. Adjust the flavors to taste.

3. To serve, divide the chickpea salad between the tortillas and top each with cherry tomatoes, Persian cucumber, and vegan feta. Drizzle with vegan tzatziki.

BBQ LENTIL TACOS

SERVES 6 Let your slow cooker do the work this Tuesday. Once you sauté the onion and garlic, all you have to do is toss the remaining ingredients into the slow cooker and enjoy the delicious aroma of your favorite BBQ sauce wafting from your kitchen. Make a cool and crunchy slaw just before serving and top your tacos with pickled jalapeños for an extra kick. This one gets messy, so bring a stack of napkins and a fork to the dinner table to scoop extra filling from your plate.

1 tablespoon (15 ml) avocado oil
½ yellow onion, chopped
3 garlic cloves, finely chopped
1½ cups (288 g) dried French lentils
1 teaspoon chili powder
2 cups (475 ml) vegetable broth
1½ cups (375 g) vegan BBQ sauce
¼ teaspoon fine sea salt

FOR THE SLAW
3 cups (255 g) coleslaw mix
2 tablespoons (28 g) vegan mayo
1 teaspoon apple cider vinegar
Pinch fine sea salt

TO SERVE
6 flour tortillas, warmed
¼ cup (60 g) pickled jalapeños (optional)

1. If you're using an Instant Pot, turn on the sauté feature. Pour the avocado oil into the bowl of the Instant Pot and allow it to heat up. If you're using a traditional slow cooker or crockpot, warm the avocado oil in a skillet on the stove over medium heat.

2. Add the onion and garlic to the hot oil and sauté for 3 to 5 minutes, stirring frequently, until the onion is soft and the garlic is fragrant.

3. Carefully transfer the cooked onion and garlic to the slow cooker. If using an Instant Pot, simply skip this step.

4. Add the dried French lentils, chili powder, vegetable broth, and BBQ sauce to the slow cooker and stir to combine. Cook the BBQ lentils on high for 5 to 6 hours or low for 8 to 9 hours.

5. When done, season the BBQ lentils with salt. Keep the slow cooker on warm until ready to serve.

6. To make the slaw: Combine the coleslaw mix, vegan mayo, vinegar, and salt in a bowl. Stir to blend.

7. To serve, spoon the BBQ lentils into the tortillas and top each with slaw and pickled jalapeño, if using.

CRISPY SHEET PAN TACOS WITH PINTO BEANS

SERVES 4 TO 5   Stuffed with seasoned veggies and pinto beans, baked in a crispy taco shell, and topped with creamy avocado mash, these sheet pan tacos are sure to satisfy even the pickiest eaters at your dinner table. The combination of flavors and textures in this recipe will have you going back for seconds every single time. Be sure to warm your tortillas before filling them so they don't crack when folded in half.

1 can (15 ounces, or 425 g) whole kernel
   sweet corn, drained
1 teaspoon avocado oil
½ yellow onion, finely chopped
4 garlic cloves, minced
1 jar (12 ounces, or 340 g) roasted red peppers,
   drained and chopped
1 can (15 ounces, or 425 g) pinto beans,
   drained and rinsed
2½ tablespoons (23 g) mild taco seasoning
½ teaspoon fine sea salt
½ cup (128 g) Salsa Verde (page 21)

FOR THE AVOCADO MASH
2 avocados
Juice of 1 lime
½ teaspoon fine sea salt

TO SERVE
10 taco-size flour tortillas
Avocado oil cooking spray

1. Preheat the oven to 400°F (200°C, or gas mark 6). Preheat a large nonstick skillet over medium heat. When the skillet is hot, add the corn and spread it out in a single layer. Allow the corn to cook for 4 to 5 minutes undisturbed, then cook for another 5 minutes, stirring occasionally and repeating until all of the corn is bright yellow and slightly charred, about 15 minutes total.

2. Drizzle a teaspoon of avocado oil into the skillet. Add the onion and garlic and sauté for 2 minutes, stirring frequently.

3. Add the roasted red pepper, pinto beans, taco seasoning, and salt to the skillet and stir to combine. Pour in the Salsa Verde and give the ingredients a final stir. Turn off the heat.

4. Warm your tortillas by wrapping them in a damp paper towel and microwaving for 15 seconds. Alternatively, you can heat them one at a time in a dry skillet over medium heat for 30 seconds on each side. This will prevent the tortillas from cracking when you fold them in half.

5. Working one at a time, spray both sides of each tortilla with avocado oil cooking spray. Spoon a few tablespoons of the veggie and bean mixture into the middle of each tortilla, then fold in half. Repeat with all of the tortillas and remaining taco filling.

6. Arrange the tacos in a single layer on a large baking sheet or split the tacos between 2 smaller baking sheets. Bake the tacos for 20 minutes. When done, they should look golden and crispy.

7. To make the avocado mash: Slice open the avocados and discard the pits. Scoop out the flesh into a small bowl and discard the peel. Use a fork to mash the avocado; it's okay if a few chunks remain. Stir in the lime juice and salt.

8. To serve, spoon the avocado mash on top of the crispy tacos.

BEAN, CHICKPEA, AND LENTIL TACOS

SWEET POTATO AND BLACK BEAN TOSTADAS

....

SERVES 4 If you have never made homemade tostadas, this recipe is a fantastic introduction. A tostada is a flat and crispy tortilla loaded with toppings and served open-faced and eaten with your hands. Tostadas can be messy to eat, but that's all part of the fun. Making your own Tostada Shells (page 18) is incredibly easy and super satisfying. These are topped with roasted sweet potatoes, seasoned black beans, avocado, Pickled Red Onion (page 27), and cilantro. Tip: Make your Pickled Red Onions ahead of time for the best flavor!

FOR THE FILLING
4 cups (532 g) sweet potatoes, peeled and cut into ½-inch
　　(1.3 cm) cubes (about 2 medium sweet potatoes)
2 tablespoons (30 ml) avocado oil
1 teaspoon fine sea salt
Freshly cracked black pepper

FOR THE BLACK BEANS
1 can (15 ounce, or 425 g) low-sodium black beans,
　　drained and lightly rinsed
1 tablespoon (8 g) Salsa Verde (page 21)
1¼ teaspoons chili powder
¼ teaspoon fine sea salt

TO SERVE
8 Tostada Shells (page 18)
2 avocados, peeled and sliced
Pickled Red Onion (page 27)
Fresh cilantro, chopped
Lime wedges

1. Preheat the oven to 350°F (180°C, or gas mark 4) and line a large baking sheet or 2 smaller baking sheets with parchment paper.

2. To make the filling: Combine the sweet potato cubes, avocado oil, salt, and pepper in a mixing bowl. Toss to coat.

3. Transfer the sweet potato cubes to the prepared baking sheet(s), making sure they're arranged in a single layer. Bake for 15 minutes, flip, then bake for 5 to 10 minutes more, until tender and lightly browned.

4. To make the black beans: Warm the black beans in a small saucepan over medium-low heat. Add the Salsa Verde, chili powder, and salt to the beans and stir. Keep the beans over low heat until you're ready to serve.

5. To serve, top each crispy tostada with black beans, roasted sweet potato cubes, avocado slices, Pickled Red Onion, and cilantro. Serve with extra lime wedges on the side.

CRISPY BAKED FALAFEL TACOS

SERVES 4 Good falafel should be crispy on the outside and fluffy and soft on the inside. Frying is the best way to achieve the perfect texture, but baking is much healthier. In this recipe, homemade falafel is baked on an oiled baking sheet to get it crispy on both sides at once. I highly recommend using dried chickpeas instead of canned for the best texture. Just remember to soak them in a bowl of water overnight!

1 cup (200 g) dried chickpeas, covered
   with water and soaked 24 hours
½ yellow onion, roughly chopped
4 garlic cloves
1 bunch fresh cilantro
1 jalapeño, cored
1½ teaspoons fine sea salt
1 tablespoon cumin
1 teaspoon ground coriander
1½ teaspoons baking powder
2 tablespoons (16 g) all-purpose flour
¼ cup (60 ml) olive oil

TO SERVE
1 container (8 ounces, or 225 g) hummus
8 fajita tortillas, warmed
Fresh arugula
Vegan Tzatziki (page 55)
Persian cucumbers, diced
Grape tomatoes, halved
Pickled Red Onion (page 27) or crispy onions

1. Drain the chickpeas and add them to the bowl of a large capacity food processor. Add the yellow onion, garlic, cilantro, jalapeño, salt, cumin, coriander, baking powder, and flour. Run the food processor until well combined and fairly smooth, pausing to scrape down the sides of the bowl as needed.

2. Scoop the falafel mixture into a bowl and refrigerate it for an hour. This step will help the falafel keep its shape while baking.

3. Preheat the oven to 400°F (200°C, or gas mark 6). Pour the olive oil onto a rimmed baking sheet and tilt it back and forth until the entire surface is evenly coated.

4. Roll the falafel mixture into golf ball–size balls and place them in rows on the prepared baking sheet. Use a spatula or the palm of your hand to gently flatten each falafel piece.

5. Bake the falafel for 25 minutes, flip each piece, and bake 10 minutes more. When it's done, the falafel will be lightly browned and crisp on both sides. When cool enough to handle, chop the falafel pieces into quarters.

6. To serve, spread a layer of hummus on each tortilla. Top with fresh arugula, falafel pieces, Vegan Tzatziki, diced cucumber, grape tomatoes, and Pickled Red Onion or crispy onions.

BEAN, CHICKPEA, AND LENTIL TACOS

SPICY PLANTAIN AND BLACK BEAN TACOS

SERVES 4   Sweet and spicy plantains join forces with seasoned black beans in this super satisfying weeknight taco recipe. Dinner comes together quickly if you make the Jalapeño Ranch (page 30) in advance. Schedule it into your weekend meal prep! Radishes and cilantro offer a delightful crunch to this warm and hearty meal.

2 ripe plantains, peeled and sliced diagonally into ¼-inch (6 mm) pieces
1 teaspoon chili powder
¼ teaspoon cayenne
1 tablespoon (9 g) coconut sugar
½ teaspoon fine sea salt
1 tablespoon (15 ml) avocado oil

FOR THE BLACK BEANS
1 teaspoon avocado oil
1 large garlic clove, grated
1 can (15 ounces, or 425 g) black beans
½ teaspoon cumin
½ teaspoon paprika
¼ teaspoon fine sea salt

TO SERVE
8 corn tortillas, warmed
Jalapeño Ranch (page 30)
1 bunch of radishes, cut into thin matchsticks
Fresh cilantro, chopped

1. Place the sliced plantains in a large mixing bowl. In a smaller bowl, whisk together the chili powder, cayenne, coconut sugar, and salt.

2. Sprinkle the spice mix over the plantains and gently stir to coat each piece.

3. Warm 1 tablespoon (15 ml) of avocado oil in a large skillet over medium-high heat. When the oil is hot, add the plantain pieces in a single layer. Cook the plantains for 3 minutes on each side, until nicely caramelized. Turn off the heat and transfer the plantains to a wire rack to cool.

4. To make the black beans: Warm 1 teaspoon of avocado oil in a small saucepan over medium heat. When the oil is hot, add the garlic and sauté for 1 minute. Pour in the black beans and season with cumin, paprika, and salt. Bring the beans to a boil, then reduce the heat to keep the beans warm, stirring occasionally.

5. To serve, divide the black beans between the tortillas. Top each with a few pieces of plantain, a drizzle of Jalapeño Ranch, sliced radish, and cilantro.

HARISSA ROASTED CAULIFLOWER AND CHICKPEA TACOS

SERVES 4   Harissa is a spicy and smoky chili paste with North African roots. It adds a wonderful flavor to protein, vegetables, and even hummus. In this recipe, harissa paste coats cauliflower and chickpeas for my favorite roasted veggie tacos. A drizzle of lemon garlic tahini sauce, crunchy cucumber, and fresh mint add layers of delicious taste and texture.

1 head cauliflower, chopped into florets
1 can (15.5 ounces, or 440 g) chickpeas,
    drained and rinsed
3 tablespoons (45 g) harissa paste, divided
1 tablespoon + 1 teaspoon (20 ml) avocado oil, divided
¼ teaspoon fine sea salt

FOR THE LEMON GARLIC TAHINI SAUCE
½ cup (120 g) tahini
¼ cup (60 ml) lemon juice
1 large garlic clove, grated
½ teaspoon fine sea salt
3 tablespoons (45 ml) filtered water,
    plus more as needed

TO SERVE
8 flour tortillas, warmed
2 Persian cucumbers, thinly sliced
1 bunch of fresh mint, torn
Pickled Red Onion (page 27)
1 lemon, cut into wedges

1. Preheat the oven to 400°F (200°C, or gas mark 6) and line 2 baking sheets with parchment paper.

2. Combine the cauliflower florets in a large mixing bowl with 2 tablespoons (30 g) of harissa paste and 1 tablespoon (15 ml) of avocado oil. Stir to coat.

3. Spread the cauliflower florets on one of the prepared baking sheets and roast for 30 minutes, flipping the pieces halfway through.

4. Dry the chickpeas on a clean kitchen towel, then transfer them to the mixing bowl you used for the cauliflower. Add the remaining 1 tablespoon (15 g) of harissa and 1 teaspoon of avocado oil. Stir to coat.

5. Spread the seasoned chickpeas on the other prepared baking sheet and slide it into the oven to join the cauliflower. Roast for 15 minutes, shaking the pan halfway through.

6. When the cauliflower and chickpeas are golden and crisp, remove both baking sheets from the oven. Spill the roasted chickpeas onto the tray of roasted cauliflower and season with salt.

7. To make the lemon garlic tahini sauce: Combine the tahini, lemon juice, garlic, fine sea salt, and water in a small bowl. Whisk until smooth, adding another teaspoon of water if needed to achieve a pourable texture.

8. To serve, divide the harissa roasted cauliflower and chickpeas between the tortillas. Top with lemon garlic tahini sauce, cucumber slices, mint, and Pickled Red Onion. Add a lemon wedge to each plate, for squeezing.

BEAN, CHICKPEA, AND LENTIL TACOS

CHIMICHURRI GRILLED VEGGIE AND WHITE BEAN TACOS

SERVES 4 Nothing screams "summer!" like grilled veggies. Whether you harvest them from your own garden or scoop them up at the farmers market, sweet corn, red bell peppers, and zucchini are at their peak of flavor and freshness from July to September. Of course, you can make this recipe any time of year that your taste buds beg for a taste of summer. This recipe highlights my favorite summer veggies and pairs them with protein-packed white beans and zesty chimichurri for a fresh and satisfying meal.

FOR THE CHIMICHURRI

1 bunch flat-leaf (Italian) parsley
1½ tablespoons (25 ml) red wine vinegar
½ teaspoon chili flakes
2 garlic cloves
⅓ cup (80 ml) + 1 tablespoon (15 ml) olive oil
½ teaspoon fine sea salt

FOR THE VEGGIES

3 ears of sweet corn, shucked
2 red bell peppers, sliced in half lengthwise, seeds removed
1 zucchini, sliced in half lengthwise
3 tablespoons (45 ml) avocado oil
1 teaspoon fine sea salt
Freshly cracked black pepper

TO SERVE

1 can (15.5 ounces, or 440 g) cannellini beans, drained and rinsed
8 taco-size flour tortillas, warmed

1. Preheat a grill or set a cast iron grill pan over medium heat for 5 to 10 minutes, until hot.

2. To make the chimichurri: Place all of the ingredients in a small blender or food processor and pulse until chunky, yet well combined. If you don't have a small blender or food processor, you can finely chop the parsley and garlic by hand with a sharp knife and combine all of the ingredients in a mixing bowl.

3. To make the veggies: Arrange the corn, red bell pepper, and zucchini on a large baking sheet for easy prep and cleanup. Drizzle with avocado oil and toss to coat. Sprinkle with salt and pepper.

4. Use tongs to transfer the veggies to the hot grill or cast iron grill pan. Cook for about 4 minutes, until you see char marks. Turn the veggies and grill for another 4 to 5 minutes, until al dente and nicely charred on all sides. Note: If using a grill pan, don't overcrowd the pan. Cook the veggies one at a time if needed.

5. Transfer the veggies to a cutting board. When cool enough to handle, cut the corn off the cob, slice the bell pepper into strips, and slice the zucchini into half-moons.

6. Pour the drained cannellini beans into a medium bowl. Add 2 tablespoons (28 g) of chimichurri and toss to coat. Reserve the remaining chimichurri for drizzling.

7. To serve, divide the cannellini beans and grilled veggies between the tortillas. Drizzle each with chimichurri.

PINTO BEAN AND AVOCADO CORN SALSA TOSTADAS

SERVES 2 TO 3   Onion, garlic, and spices (along with a little bit of effort) can take an ordinary can of pinto beans from blah to restaurant-quality in less than 20 minutes. Creamy, seasoned pinto beans make up the core of this recipe, so we want them as flavorful as they can be. Pile your tostada high with avocado corn salsa for a Tuesday night meal that is equal parts fresh and satisfying.

2 teaspoons avocado oil
½ cup (80 g) finely chopped yellow onion
2 garlic cloves, finely chopped
1 can (15 ounces, or 425 g) pinto beans
½ teaspoon cumin
½ teaspoon oregano
½ teaspoon fine sea salt
Pinch cayenne
½ cup (120 ml) water
1 bay leaf

FOR THE AVOCADO CORN SALSA
1 cup (154 g) fresh corn kernels
½ red bell pepper, finely chopped
½ cup (80 g) finely chopped red onion
½ cup (8 g) finely chopped fresh cilantro
½ jalapeño, finely chopped
2 avocados, peeled and diced small
1 teaspoon fine sea salt
Juice and zest of 1 lime

TO SERVE
6 Tostada Shells (page 18)
Pickled Red Onion (page 27)

1. Warm the avocado oil in a small saucepan over medium heat. When the oil is hot, add the onion and garlic. Sauté for 3 minutes, until soft and fragrant.

2. Drain the pinto beans but don't rinse them. Pour the pinto beans and any remaining liquid into the saucepan.

3. Add the cumin, oregano, salt, and cayenne and stir to combine.

4. Pour the water into the saucepan and add the bay leaf. Bring to a boil, then reduce the heat to maintain a gentle simmer for 15 minutes. Toward the end of cooking, mash half of the beans with the tip of a wooden spoon or spatula.

5. To make the avocado corn salsa: Combine all of the ingredients in a large mixing bowl and stir to blend.

6. To serve, remove the bay leaf and spoon the beans onto crispy tostada shells. Top each with avocado corn salsa and Pickled Red Onion.

SMOKY LENTIL TACOS WITH AVOCADO

SERVES 4   Smoky, spiced lentils lend crumbly and tender texture to this one-pot taco recipe. The lentil taco "meat" is made with ingredients you probably already have on your spice rack and in your pantry. Thinly shredded romaine lettuce, pico de gallo, and sliced avocado make perfect toppings and add fresh flavor. My favorite way to eat these tacos is to stuff as much as I can into warm corn tortillas and eat everything that falls onto my plate with a fork.

1 tablespoon (15 ml) avocado oil
½ cup (80 g) finely chopped yellow onion
3 garlic cloves, finely chopped
1 teaspoon smoked paprika
1 teaspoon cumin
1½ teaspoons chili powder
½ teaspoon fine sea salt
1 cup (192 g) dried lentils
2 cups (475 ml) vegetable broth
2 teaspoons low-sodium soy sauce
1 tablespoon (16 g) tomato paste
1 tablespoon (15 ml) sauce from a can of chipotle
   peppers in adobo
½ cup (60 g) finely chopped raw walnuts

TO SERVE
8 corn tortillas, warmed
Romaine lettuce, shredded
1 cup (240 g) pico de gallo
1 avocado, peeled and thinly sliced

1. Warm the avocado oil in a saucepan over medium heat. When the oil is hot, add the onion and garlic. Sauté until soft and fragrant, about 3 minutes.

2. Sprinkle the smoked paprika, cumin, chili powder, and salt over the onion and garlic and stir. Sauté for 2 minutes more.

3. Pour the lentils and vegetable broth into the pot. Add the soy sauce, tomato paste, and adobo sauce. Stir to combine and turn the heat to medium-high.

4. When the liquid reaches a boil, cover the saucepan and turn the heat to medium-low. Simmer the lentils covered for 20 minutes.

5. Remove the lid and continue to simmer uncovered until most of the liquid has cooked off. Stir the chopped walnuts into the lentils and turn off the heat.

6. To serve, divide the smoky lentil taco filling between the tortillas. Top with shredded romaine, pico de gallo, and sliced avocado.

> **CHAPTER 4** <

CAULIFLOWER, CORN, AND POTATO TACOS

Cauliflower, corn, and potatoes deserve a chapter all their own. Cauliflower in particular makes a fantastic taco filling because it's practically flavorless and takes on the flavor of whatever spices or sauce it is coated with. When dunked in batter and baked, like in Buffalo Cauliflower Tacos with Jalapeño Ranch (page 84), cauliflower takes on a satisfying, chewy texture. In Cauliflower Walnut Tacos (page 91), cauliflower is pulsed with walnuts and roasted with spicy sauce to become a crumbly taco "meat" perfect for pairing with classic toppings.

Corn, potatoes, and sweet potatoes carry the recipes in the rest of this chapter, featuring some unexpected flavor pairings and ingredients. Roasted Corn and Poblano Tacos (page 83) take advantage of fresh summer produce while Mexican-Style Street Corn Tacos (page 79) offer a taste of Mexican-inspired street food. I highly recommend using fresh corn when possible, but canned corn is a great alternative in the off season.

BLACKENED CAULIFLOWER TACOS WITH CHIPOTLE AIOLI

SERVES 4 Cauliflower makes a fantastic taco filling because it is extremely versatile and can take on nearly any flavor profile. In this recipe, cauliflower is coated in blackening spices and roasted until crisp and nearly charred. A simple citrus slaw offers a pleasant crunch while chipotle aioli turns up the heat. For a less spicy Chipotle Aioli (page 26), use fewer chipotle peppers or dial up the maple syrup a touch.

1 head cauliflower, cut into small florets
2 tablespoons (30 ml) avocado oil
2 tablespoons (18 g) blackening or Cajun seasoning

FOR THE SLAW
2 cups (140 g) shredded red cabbage
2 cups (220 g) shredded carrot
½ cup (8 g) finely chopped fresh cilantro
1 tablespoon (15 ml) avocado oil
Juice of ½ lime (1 tablespoon [15 ml])
½ teaspoon fine sea salt

TO SERVE
8 flour tortillas, warmed
Chipotle Aioli (page 26)

1. Preheat the oven to 425°F (220°C, or gas mark 7) and line a large baking sheet with parchment paper or a silicone baking mat.

2. Transfer the cauliflower florets to the baking sheet. Drizzle with 2 tablespoons (30 ml) of avocado oil and sprinkle the blackening or Cajun seasoning over the cauliflower. Toss to coat.

3. Roast for 30 minutes, flipping the pieces halfway through to ensure even cooking. When done, the cauliflower should be golden and lightly charred on the edges.

4. To make the slaw: Combine the red cabbage, carrot, and cilantro in a bowl. Drizzle 1 tablespoon (15 ml) of avocado oil over the shredded vegetables. Add the lime juice and salt; toss to combine.

5. To serve, divide the blackened cauliflower between the tortillas and top with the slaw. Serve the Chipotle Aioli on the side or drizzle over the tacos.

MEXICAN-STYLE STREET CORN TACOS

SERVES 4 Esquites are a popular corn-based snack often served in a cup and sold by street vendors in Mexico. Traditional esquites are made with fresh corn, mayonnaise, cilantro, chili powder, lime, and Cotija cheese. This plant-based version is my take on the original—minus the dairy—and the result is incredibly satisfying. I recommend using street taco–size tortillas for the best filling-to-tortilla ratio.

1 tablespoon (15 ml) avocado oil

4 ears of fresh corn, shucked and kernels removed (or 2 cans [15 ounces, or 425 g each] corn, drained)

2 scallions, thinly sliced (keep the dark green parts separate from the light green and white parts)

3 tablespoons (42 g) vegan mayo

Juice of 1 lime

1 jalapeño, finely chopped

½ red bell pepper, finely chopped

¼ cup (4 g) fresh cilantro

1 teaspoon chili powder

¼ teaspoon fine sea salt

TO SERVE

12 street taco–size flour tortillas, warmed

½ cup (45 g) vegan feta (optional)

1. Heat the avocado oil in a large skillet over medium-high heat.

2. When the oil is hot, add the corn to the skillet and spread it out in an even layer. Allow the corn to cook undisturbed for 3 to 4 minutes, then stir.

3. Repeat this process until the corn is bright yellow and golden in some spots, about 10 minutes. Add the light green and white parts of the scallion to the pan and sauté for 1 minute more. Turn off the heat.

4. Transfer the cooked corn and scallions into a large mixing bowl. Add the vegan mayo, lime juice, jalapeño, red bell pepper, cilantro, chili powder, and the dark green parts of the scallion. Season with salt and stir to combine all of the ingredients.

5. To serve, divide the corn mixture between the tortillas and garnish with vegan feta, if using.

CURRIED POTATO AND CAULIFLOWER TACOS

....

SERVES 3 TO 4 Fragrant curry powder makes ordinary potatoes and cauliflower sing with flavor in this veggie-forward taco. Ground spices lose their flavor and aroma quickly, so if your jar of curry powder is more than six months old, I highly recommend replacing it for the best taste. Cilantro lime slaw and Pickled Red Onion (page 27) provide a cool, crunchy texture contrast that make this taco one of my favorites.

12 ounces (340 g) gold potatoes, cut into
  ½-inch (1.3 cm) cubes
12 ounces (340 g) cauliflower, cut into small florets
2 tablespoons (30 ml) avocado oil
1½ teaspoons curry powder
½ teaspoon fine sea salt
Freshly cracked black pepper

FOR THE CILANTRO LIME SLAW
½ cup (115 g) vegan mayo
1 tablespoon (15 ml) lime juice
1 large garlic clove, grated
¼ teaspoon fine sea salt
⅓ cup (5 g) finely chopped fresh cilantro
4 cups (280 g) shredded green cabbage

TO SERVE
8 corn tortillas, warmed
Pickled Red Onion (page 27)
Fresh cilantro, chopped

1. If using an oven instead of an air fryer, preheat oven to 400°F (200°C, or gas mark 6). Combine the potatoes and cauliflower florets in a mixing bowl. Add the avocado oil, curry powder, salt, and pepper. Toss to coat.

2. Transfer the potatoes and cauliflower to an air fryer. You may need to air fry in batches, as to not overcrowd the basket. The potatoes and cauliflower need space to get crispy.

3. Air fry the potatoes and cauliflower for 18 to 20 minutes, shaking the basket or stirring halfway through. To roast your vegetables in the oven, arrange them in a single layer on a baking sheet lined with parchment paper. Bake for 20 minutes, flipping halfway through. When done, the potatoes and cauliflower should be golden and crisp on the edges.

4. To make the cilantro lime slaw: In the bowl you used to prepare the vegetables, combine the vegan mayo, lime juice, garlic, salt, and cilantro. Add the shredded cabbage to the bowl and toss to coat.

5. To serve, divide the cilantro lime slaw between the tortillas. Top with the curried potato and cauliflower, Pickled Red Onion, and cilantro.

ROASTED CORN AND POBLANO TACOS

....

SERVES 4   If you typically default to bell peppers, this recipe will nudge you out of your comfort zone. Poblano peppers are ever so slightly spicier than bell peppers but nowhere near as hot as jalapeños. They roast up beautifully and tuck into soft corn tortillas with roasted corn, avocado, and scallions. I love topping these tacos with fresh cilantro and a dollop of vegan sour cream.

6 ears of sweet corn, husks removed
1 teaspoon chipotle chili powder
½ teaspoon garlic powder
½ teaspoon onion powder
¼ teaspoon cumin
¼ teaspoon fine sea salt
1½ tablespoons (25 ml) avocado oil, divided
2 poblano peppers
1 avocado, peeled and diced
2 scallions, thinly sliced
Zest of 1 lime and juice of ½ lime (1 tablespoon, or 15 ml)

TO SERVE
8 flour tortillas, warmed
Fresh cilantro, chopped
Vegan sour cream

1. Preheat the oven to 425°F (220°C, or gas mark 7) and line 2 baking sheets with parchment paper.

2. Slice the kernels off the ears of corn and transfer to a medium bowl.

3. In a small bowl, combine the chipotle chili powder, garlic powder, onion powder, cumin, and salt. Stir to blend.

4. Drizzle the corn with 1 tablespoon (15 ml) of avocado oil and sprinkle with the spice mix. Toss to coat.

5. Spread the corn kernels in an even layer on one of the baking sheets. Place the poblano peppers on the other baking sheet and coat with the remaining ½ tablespoon (7.5 ml) of avocado oil.

6. Roast for 20 to 25 minutes, stirring the corn and flipping the peppers halfway through. When done, the peppers and corn should be lightly charred and tender, but not soft or mushy.

7. When the corn has cooled, transfer it to a bowl with the avocado and scallions. Sprinkle in the lime zest and add the lime juice. Stir to combine.

8. When the peppers have cooled, peel the skin and remove the stem. Scrape out the seeds and discard. Slice the peppers into ½-inch (1.3 cm) strips.

9. To serve, divide the roasted poblano peppers between the tortillas. Top with the corn and avocado mixture, cilantro, and vegan sour cream.

CAULIFLOWER, CORN, AND POTATO TACOS

BUFFALO CAULIFLOWER TACOS WITH JALAPEÑO RANCH

SERVES 4   Buffalo cauliflower wings are a plant-based classic. Here, they get wrapped up in a soft tortilla and drizzled with cool Jalapeño Ranch (page 30) made from blended cashews and avocado. Fresh cilantro and shredded veggies offer a satisfying crunch and bring balance to what just might be the spiciest taco recipe in this cookbook.

1 head cauliflower
1½ cups (188 g) all-purpose flour
1 teaspoon garlic powder
½ teaspoon fine sea salt
1½ cups (355 ml) filtered water
1 cup (235 ml) hot sauce
¼ cup (60 ml) olive oil
1 teaspoon maple syrup

TO SERVE
Shredded cabbage
Shredded carrot
8 flour or corn tortillas, warmed
Jalapeño Ranch (page 30)
Fresh cilantro, chopped (optional)

1. Preheat the oven to 375°F (190°C, or gas mark 5) and line 2 large baking sheets with parchment paper or silicone baking mats.

2. Chop the head of cauliflower into florets. Cut them a bit smaller than you normally would so they tuck nicely into the tortillas.

3. Combine the all-purpose flour, garlic powder, and salt in a mixing bowl. Whisk in the water until all of the dry ingredients are absorbed. The batter should resemble pancake batter when fully mixed.

4. In a separate bowl, combine the hot sauce, olive oil, and maple syrup; set aside.

5. Place the cauliflower florets in the bowl of batter and gently stir so each piece is coated. Using a slotted spoon, scoop up the battered cauliflower and transfer it to the baking sheets, leaving excess batter behind in the bowl. Arrange the cauliflower in a single layer with space between each piece for even cooking.

6. Bake the cauliflower for 15 minutes on the middle rack of the oven.

7. Remove the cauliflower from the oven and carefully transfer it to the bowl of hot sauce.

8. Gently stir to coat each piece of cauliflower, then use a slotted spoon to transfer the cauliflower back onto the baking sheets.

9. Bake the cauliflower for another 5 to 7 minutes, until the hot sauce has set and the cauliflower looks lightly golden.

10. To serve, divide the shredded cabbage and carrots between the tortillas and top with buffalo cauliflower. Drizzle the Jalapeño Ranch over the tacos or serve it in a small pitcher for everyone to dress their own. Sprinkle the tacos with cilantro, if desired.

SPICY POTATO TACOS

SERVES 4 We regularly eat breakfast for dinner in my family, so it felt appropriate to include my favorite breakfast taco recipe in this book. Potatoes and onions are crisped in the air fryer and layered in soft flour tortillas with seasoned black beans, Chipotle Aioli, and sliced avocado. This is easily in my top five favorite taco recipes of all time.

5 medium gold potatoes, about 5 ounces (140 g) each, diced

1 small yellow onion, diced

1½ tablespoons (25 ml) avocado oil

1 teaspoon fine sea salt

Freshly cracked black pepper

1 can (15 ounces, or 425 g) low-sodium black beans, drained and rinsed

½ teaspoon chili powder

¼ teaspoon fine sea salt

TO SERVE

4 soft flour tortillas, warmed

1 avocado, peeled and sliced

Fresh cilantro, for garnish

Chipotle Aioli (page 26)

Lime wedges

1. Combine the potatoes and onion in a bowl. Drizzle with avocado oil and season with salt and pepper; toss to coat.

2. Transfer the potatoes and onions to the basket of an air fryer. Air fry the potatoes and onions at 375°F (190°C, or gas mark 5) for 20 minutes, pausing to shake the basket every 7 to 8 minutes so the potatoes crisp evenly.

3. Warm the black beans in a small saucepan over medium-low heat. Season with chili powder and salt.

4. To serve, divide the crispy potatoes and black beans between the tortillas. Top with avocado slices and cilantro and drizzle with Chipotle Aioli. Serve each taco with a lime wedge.

BANG BANG CAULIFLOWER TACOS

SERVES 4 TO 6   These tacos combine some of my favorite flavors and textures. Crispy breaded cauliflower is wrapped in soft corn tortillas and topped with a creamy, sweet, and spicy sauce. Shredded cabbage and scallions lend a delightful crunch! The term "bang bang" refers to the sticky, spicy sauce that coats the cauliflower and was inspired by the popular shrimp dish that is a staple on many restaurant menus.

1 head cauliflower
1½ cups (188 g) all-purpose flour
1 teaspoon garlic powder
½ teaspoon onion powder
2 teaspoons paprika
½ teaspoon fine sea salt
1½ cups (355 ml) filtered water
Avocado oil cooking spray

FOR THE BANG BANG SAUCE
½ cup (115 g) vegan mayo
2 tablespoons (40 g) sweet chili sauce
½ teaspoon rice vinegar
1½ teaspoons sriracha
Water, as needed

TO SERVE
Green and red cabbage, shredded
3 scallions, sliced
12 corn tortillas, warmed

1. Preheat the oven to 400°F (200°C, or gas mark 6) and line 2 large baking sheets with parchment paper or silicone baking mats.

2. Chop the head of cauliflower into florets. Cut them a bit smaller than you normally would so they tuck nicely into the tortillas.

3. Combine the all-purpose flour, garlic powder, onion powder, paprika, and salt in a mixing bowl. Whisk in the water until all of the dry ingredients are absorbed. The batter should resemble thick pancake batter when fully mixed.

4. Place the cauliflower florets in the bowl of batter and gently stir so each piece is coated. Using a slotted spoon, scoop up the battered cauliflower and transfer it to the baking sheets, leaving excess batter behind in the bowl. Arrange the cauliflower in a single layer with space between each piece for even cooking.

5. Bake the cauliflower for 15 minutes on the middle rack of the oven. Spray with avocado oil cooking spray, then bake for 10 minutes more. Remove the cauliflower from the oven and set aside.

6. To make the bang bang sauce: In a medium bowl, mix together the vegan mayo, sweet chili sauce, rice vinegar, and sriracha. Add a splash of water if needed to reach a drizzling consistency.

7. To serve, divide shredded cabbage and scallions between the tortillas. Top with the baked cauliflower and drizzle each with a generous amount of bang bang sauce.

CAULIFLOWER WALNUT TACOS

SERVES 4 TO 5   If cauliflower and walnut sounds like a weird combination for taco filling, I challenge you to try this recipe. When ground up and combined with sauce from a can of chipotle peppers in adobo sauce and taco seasoning, the mixture makes a fantastic base for your favorite taco toppings. I kept it classic with romaine lettuce, pico de gallo, and vegan sour cream. Feel free to swap out or add your favorite garnishes to make this recipe a staple recipe you'll come back to often.

4 cups (400 g) cauliflower florets
2 cups (200 g) walnuts
3 tablespoons (45 ml) sauce from a can of chipotle
    peppers in adobo sauce
2 tablespoons (30 ml) avocado oil
2 tablespoons (18 g) taco seasoning

TO SERVE
10 soft corn tortillas, warmed
2 cups (94 g) shredded romaine lettuce
1 cup (240 g) pico de gallo
Vegan sour cream
Lime wedges

1. Preheat the oven to 375°F (190°C, or gas mark 5) and line a large baking sheet with parchment paper.

2. Combine the cauliflower florets, walnuts, the adobo sauce, avocado oil, and taco seasoning in a large capacity food processor and pulse until finely chopped and mixed together, but not puréed. If the food processor is small, work in batches.

3. Spread the mixture in an even layer on the prepared baking sheet. Bake the cauliflower walnut taco "meat" for 25 to 30 minutes, stirring every 10 minutes, until golden brown and slightly crispy on the edges.

4. To serve, arrange the tortillas on a serving platter or divide between plates. Layer each with romaine lettuce, cauliflower walnut taco filling, and pico de gallo. Drizzle with vegan sour cream and offer lime wedges on the side.

CRISPY BBQ CAULIFLOWER TACOS

SERVES 4   This taco recipe is a BBQ lover's dream. The best part is that you can make it your own with your favorite vegan BBQ sauce—there are so many flavorful varieties available! I prefer to bread and bake my cauliflower florets before coating them in BBQ sauce to get a chewy, winglike texture. A drizzle of vegan ranch dressing, shredded lettuce, and some crispy onions make this recipe really dynamic and flavorful.

½ head cauliflower
¾ cup (94 g) all-purpose flour
½ teaspoon garlic powder
¼ teaspoon fine sea salt
¾ cup (175 ml) filtered water
1 cup (250 g) vegan BBQ sauce

TO SERVE
8 corn tortillas, warmed
Shredded lettuce
Vegan ranch dressing
Crispy onions

1. Preheat the oven to 400°F (200°C, or gas mark 6) and line 2 large baking sheets with parchment paper.

2. Chop the head of cauliflower into florets. Cut them a bit smaller than you normally would so they tuck nicely into the tortillas.

3. Combine the all-purpose flour, garlic powder, and salt in a mixing bowl. Whisk in the water until all of the dry ingredients are absorbed. The batter should resemble pancake batter when fully mixed.

4. Place the cauliflower florets in the bowl of batter and gently stir so each piece is coated.

5. Use a slotted spoon to transfer the cauliflower to the baking sheets, leaving excess batter behind in the bowl. Arrange the cauliflower in a single layer with space between each piece for even cooking.

6. Bake the cauliflower for 15 minutes, until golden and slightly crisp.

7. Remove the cauliflower from the oven and carefully transfer it to a bowl containing the BBQ sauce.

8. Gently stir to coat each piece of cauliflower, then use a slotted spoon to transfer the cauliflower back to the baking sheets.

9. Bake the cauliflower for another 5 to 7 minutes, until the BBQ sauce has set and caramelized slightly.

10. To serve, divide the BBQ cauliflower between the tortillas. Top with shredded lettuce, vegan ranch dressing, and crispy onions.

SPICY PEANUT SWEET POTATO TACOS

SERVES 4 TO 5   I could eat this Asian-inspired taco recipe every Tuesday of the year. It's that good! The secret is in the sauce. Tender roasted sweet potatoes are wrapped up in flour tortillas along with crunchy cabbage, cilantro, and peanuts. A generous drizzle of spicy peanut sauce sends the flavor of these plant-based tacos over the top. Tip: Double the peanut sauce recipe and enjoy it again later in the week with rice noodles, tofu, and veggies.

2 medium sweet potatoes, peeled
2 tablespoons (30 ml) avocado oil
1 teaspoon fine sea salt
Freshly cracked black pepper

FOR THE SPICY PEANUT SAUCE
⅓ cup (87 g) creamy salted peanut butter
2 tablespoons (30 ml) low-sodium soy sauce
1 tablespoon (15 ml) rice vinegar
Juice of ½ lime (1 tablespoon, or 15 ml)
1 tablespoon (15 ml) maple syrup
3 tablespoons (45 ml) water, plus more as needed
1 teaspoon sriracha
1 garlic clove, pressed or grated

FOR THE CABBAGE MIXTURE
½ cup (8 g) chopped fresh cilantro
2 cups (140 g) shredded red cabbage
2 cups (140 g) shredded green cabbage
Juice of ½ lime (1 tablespoon, or 15 ml)

TO SERVE
10 flour tortillas, warmed
½ cup (75 g) roasted peanuts, roughly chopped

1. Preheat the oven to 425°F (220°C, or gas mark 7) and line a large baking sheet with parchment paper.

2. Cut the sweet potatoes into ½-inch (1.3 cm) cubes and transfer them to a mixing bowl. Drizzle with avocado oil and sprinkle with salt and pepper. Toss to coat.

3. Transfer the sweet potato cubes onto the baking sheet and spread them in an even layer. Roast for 30 minutes, flipping halfway through. When done, the sweet potato cubes should be tender and golden on the edges.

4. To make the spicy peanut sauce: Combine all of the ingredients in a medium bowl and whisk with a fork until well combined, adding a splash of water if needed to keep the consistency drizzly.

5. Before serving, combine the cilantro, cabbage, and lime juice in a medium bowl and toss to combine.

6. To serve, divide the cabbage mixture between the tortillas. Top each with roasted sweet potato cubes, drizzle with spicy peanut sauce, and sprinkle with chopped peanuts.

CAULIFLOWER, CORN, AND POTATO TACOS

STICKY SESAME GINGER CAULIFLOWER TACOS

SERVES 4 Roasted cauliflower is the perfect vehicle for sticky sesame ginger sauce in this Asian-inspired taco recipe. The tender florets take on a winglike texture when coated in batter before getting toasty in the oven. The sauce is savory, yet mild, making this a great way to explore new flavors and textures with younger kids. If you like spicy food as much as I do, a drizzle of chili crisp just before serving dials up the heat.

FOR THE CAULIFLOWER
1 head cauliflower
1½ cups (188 g) all-purpose flour
½ teaspoon fine sea salt
1½ cups (355 ml) filtered water

FOR THE SESAME GINGER SAUCE
½ cup (120 ml) low-sodium soy sauce
¼ cup (60 ml) maple syrup
2 tablespoons (30 ml) toasted sesame oil
2 tablespoons (30 ml) rice vinegar
1½ tablespoons (12 g) ginger, peeled and grated
3 garlic cloves, grated
2 tablespoons (16 g) toasted sesame seeds

TO SERVE
8 flour tortillas, warmed
3 scallions, thinly sliced
Chili crisp (optional)

1. Preheat the oven to 375°F (190°C, or gas mark 5) and line 2 large baking sheets with parchment paper.

2. Chop the head of cauliflower into florets. Cut them a bit smaller than you normally would so they tuck nicely into the tortillas.

3. Combine the all-purpose flour and salt in a mixing bowl. Whisk in the filtered water until all of the dry ingredients are absorbed. The batter should resemble pancake batter when fully mixed.

4. Place the cauliflower florets in the bowl of batter and gently stir so each piece is coated. Using a slotted spoon, scoop up the battered cauliflower and transfer it to the baking sheets, leaving excess batter behind in the bowl. Arrange the cauliflower in a single layer with space between each piece for even cooking.

5. Bake the cauliflower for 15 minutes on the middle rack of the oven, until just barely golden.

6. While the cauliflower bakes, make the sesame ginger sauce: Whisk all of the ingredients together in a glass jar or mixing bowl.

7. Pour the sesame ginger sauce into a small saucepan and turn to medium heat. Bring the sauce to a boil, then reduce the heat to maintain a gentle simmer for 10 minutes. When done, the sauce should be reduced and slightly thickened.

8. Transfer the baked cauliflower to a heat-safe bowl. Pour the sesame ginger sauce over the cauliflower, reserving about a third of the sauce for serving. Gently stir to coat each piece.

9. Use a slotted spoon to transfer the coated cauliflower back to the baking sheets, leaving excess sauce behind in the bowl.

10. Bake the cauliflower for another 10 to 15 minutes, until the sauce is caramelized, but not burnt.

11. Return the baked cauliflower to the bowl and drizzle with the leftover sesame ginger sauce. Stir gently to coat.

12. To serve, divide the sticky sesame ginger cauliflower between the tortillas. Top with sliced scallion and chili crisp for a spicy kick, if desired.

> ❯ **CHAPTER 5** ❮

PLANT-POWERED PROTEIN TACOS

When it comes to plant-based proteins, tofu was my first love. I know tofu can be polarizing, but I hope you will give it a chance with the tacos in this chapter. I've started with my family's favorite—Baja Tofu Tacos with Citrus Crema (page 100). A surprising ingredient gives the batter a fluffy, crispy, melt-in-your-mouth texture, and the citrus crema is refreshingly bright and fun. You'll also experiment with shredding tofu in Tofu Carnitas Tacos with Apple Salsa (page 118).

Tempeh and soy chorizo share the spotlight with tofu as fabulous plant-powered proteins. Tempeh requires a quick steam bath to reduce its natural bitterness and improve the flavor—don't skip this step! Soy chorizo is my go-to protein when I'm really short on time. There is no chopping, marinating, or prep. Just squeeze it into a hot pan, like in Soy Chorizo Tacos with Mango Salsa (page 114), for a super quick Taco Tuesday dinner.

BAJA TOFU TACOS WITH CITRUS CREMA

SERVES 4 My husband could not believe he was eating tofu when he took a bite of this taco for the first time. The tofu is marinated then dunked in a fluffy batter before being fried to crispy perfection. If you feel adventurous, try swapping the sparkling water for Mexican beer in the batter for even more flavor. Drizzle your tacos with citrus crema and garnish with shredded cabbage, cilantro, and pickled jalapeño.

1 package (16 ounces, or 455 g) super-firm tofu

FOR THE MARINADE
1 tablespoon (15 ml) lime juice
1 tablespoon (15 ml) orange juice
1 tablespoon (15 ml) avocado oil
1 teaspoon chili powder
½ teaspoon cumin
½ teaspoon garlic powder
½ teaspoon fine sea salt

FOR THE BATTER
1½ cups (188 g) all-purpose flour, divided
1 teaspoon garlic powder
1 teaspoon onion powder
1 teaspoon paprika
½ teaspoon fine sea salt
½ teaspoon baking powder
1 cup (235 ml) plain sparkling water, plus more as needed
Oil, for frying

FOR THE CITRUS CREMA
¼ cup (60 g) vegan mayo
¼ cup (60 g) vegan sour cream
1 tablespoon (15 ml) lime juice
1 tablespoon (15 ml) orange juice
Zest of 1 lime
Zest of 1 orange
¼ teaspoon fine sea salt

TO SERVE
Shredded cabbage
12 corn or flour tortillas, warmed
Fresh cilantro
Pickled jalapeños

Recipe continued on page 102.

Recipe continued from page 100.

1. Drain the tofu and wrap it in a few layers of paper towels. Wrap a clean kitchen towel around the paper towels and press out as much water as possible.

2. Set the block of tofu on a cutting board, hold your knife parallel to the cutting board, and slice the block of tofu in half. Then create 5 cuts across the top of the block of tofu lengthwise to create 12 strips of equal size.

3. To make the marinade: Combine the lime juice, orange juice, avocado oil, chili powder, cumin, garlic powder, and salt in a shallow dish or zip top bag.

4. Place the tofu slices in the dish or zip top bag and flip to coat each piece. Set aside.

5. To make the batter: Combine 1 cup (125 g) of all-purpose flour with the garlic powder, onion powder, paprika, salt, and baking powder in a large bowl. Pour the carbonated water into the dry ingredients and whisk to combine. The mixture should resemble pancake batter. If it looks too dry, add another splash of carbonated water.

6. Sift the remaining ½ cup (63 g) of all-purpose flour onto a plate.

7. Pour about ¼ inch (6 mm) of oil into a small skillet and turn the heat to medium high. You'll know the oil is hot enough when a small bit of batter sizzles when it hits the pan.

8. Set up an assembly line with the tofu, the plate of flour, and the bowl of batter. Working one piece at a time, coat the tofu in a light layer of flour, then dredge it through the batter, allowing excess to drip back into the bowl. Carefully place the battered tofu in the hot oil. Cook for 3 minutes, until golden and crisp, then flip and cook 3 minutes more. Transfer to a plate to cool.

9. To make the citrus crema: Combine all of the ingredients in a small bowl. Adjust the flavors to taste.

10. To serve, add a small handful of shredded cabbage to each tortilla. Top with cilantro, pickled jalapeño, and citrus crema. Add a piece of crispy tofu to each taco and enjoy immediately.

GRILLED TOFU AND PINEAPPLE TACOS

SERVES 4 If you're used to pan frying or baking tofu, this is a great introduction to grilling your favorite plant-based protein. You can make this recipe on the stovetop or on an outdoor grill. Either way, I recommend using a cast iron grill pan for both the tofu and pineapple to get those beautiful char marks. Shredded red cabbage, Jalapeño Ranch (page 30), and fresh cilantro offer delightful brightness and crunch.

1 block (16 ounces, or 455 g) extra-firm tofu
1 pineapple
Juice and zest of 1 lime

FOR THE MARINADE
½ teaspoon paprika
½ teaspoon cumin
¼ teaspoon garlic powder
Pinch fine sea salt
1 tablespoon (15 ml) low-sodium soy sauce
1 tablespoon (15 ml) avocado oil, plus more as needed

TO SERVE
Red cabbage, shredded
8 corn tortillas, warmed
Jalapeño Ranch (page 30)
Fresh cilantro, finely chopped

1. Drain the tofu and wrap it in a few layers of paper towels. Wrap a clean kitchen towel around the paper towels and press out as much water as possible.

2. Slice the tofu into pieces ½-inch (1.3 cm) wide and 2 inches (5 cm) long. Place the tofu in a large bowl and set aside.

3. To make the marinade: Combine the paprika, cumin, garlic powder, salt, low-sodium soy sauce, and avocado oil in a small bowl. Stir to mix the ingredients together.

Recipe continued on page 105.

Recipe continued from page 103.

4. Pour the marinade over the tofu and gently toss with a silicone spatula to coat the pieces evenly. Set the tofu aside to marinate for at least 15 minutes.

5. Meanwhile, slice the pineapple. Chop off the top of the pineapple, then stand it upright on the cutting board. Use a sharp knife to slice downward all the way around the pineapple, removing the tough outer skin.

6. Avoiding the inner core of the pineapple, cut the fruit from top to bottom. Then slice those pieces into ½-inch (1.3 cm) wedges. Repeat on the other sides of the pineapple and discard the core.

7. Rub a thin layer of avocado oil into the surface of a cast iron grill pan and set it on the stovetop over medium-high heat.

8. When the pan is very hot, use tongs to lift the tofu out of the marinade and onto the pan. Arrange the tofu pieces in a single layer with a bit of space between each one. If the grill pan is small, you may need to work in batches to not overcrowd the pan.

9. Grill the tofu for 3 minutes on each side, flipping each piece when the tofu is deep golden and has grill marks. Set the grilled tofu aside on a plate.

10. Place the pineapple slices on the hot grill pan in a single layer and grill for 3 minutes on each side, until caramelized and lightly charred. Work in batches if the grill pan is small.

11. Transfer the pineapple slices to a plate. Squeeze the lime juice over the pineapple slices and sprinkle with lime zest.

12. To serve, add some shredded cabbage to the center of each tortilla. Top with grilled tofu and pineapple pieces. Drizzle with Jalapeño Ranch and garnish with cilantro.

TERIYAKI TEMPEH TACOS WITH PINEAPPLE SALSA

SERVES 4   Like tofu, tempeh takes on the flavor of the sauce or marinade it is cooked in. Tempeh has a firm, yet chewy texture that plays perfectly in plant-based tacos. If you haven't tried tempeh, this recipe presents a fabulous opportunity. Here, tempeh is crumbled and sautéed with a teriyaki-style sauce until sticky and caramelized. Topped with pineapple salsa, the sweet and spicy flavors of this Hawaiian-inspired taco will tickle your tastebuds in the best possible way.

2 packages (8 ounces, or 225 g each) tempeh, sliced into ½-inch (1.3 cm) strips
1 tablespoon (15 ml) avocado oil, for cooking

FOR THE SAUCE
½ cup (120 ml) low-sodium soy sauce
¼ cup (36 g) coconut sugar
Juice of ½ lime (1 tablespoon, or 15 ml)
1 tablespoon (8 g) fresh ginger, grated
1 large garlic clove, grated

FOR THE PINEAPPLE SALSA
2 cups (310 g) diced pineapple
½ cup (80 g) finely diced red onion
Juice of ½ lime (1 tablespoon, or 15 ml)
¼ cup (4 g) fresh cilantro
1 jalapeño, seeded and finely chopped
¼ teaspoon fine sea salt

TO SERVE
8 flour tortillas, warmed
Fresh cilantro

1. Coat the bottom of a large skillet with water and bring it to a simmer over medium heat.

2. Carefully arrange the tempeh slices in a single layer so each is making contact with the water. Cover the skillet and steam the tempeh for 10 minutes.

3. To make the sauce: In a bowl, combine the low-sodium soy sauce, coconut sugar, lime juice, ginger, and garlic. Stir to dissolve the coconut sugar in the liquid.

4. Remove the tempeh pieces from the skillet and set aside to cool. Carefully pat the tempeh with paper towels to remove any leftover moisture. Wipe the skillet dry.

5. When the tempeh is cool enough to handle, use your hands to crumble it into small pieces.

6. Heat the avocado oil in the same skillet you used to steam the tempeh. When the oil is hot, add the crumbled tempeh pieces to the pan. Cook for 8 to 10 minutes, stirring frequently, until the tempeh is lightly golden on the edges.

7. Pour the sauce over the tempeh and stir so it soaks up all of the liquid. Continue to sauté the tempeh for 5 to 6 minutes, until the pieces look slightly caramelized. Turn off the heat.

8. To make the pineapple salsa: Combine all of the ingredients in a bowl and toss to combine.

9. To serve, spoon the warm tempeh into the tortillas and top with pineapple salsa.

SHEET PAN TOFU AND FAJITA VEGGIE TACOS

SERVES 4   This recipe is in my top five favorites. I love a sheet pan meal because prep, cooking, and cleanup are so easy. This taco recipe is no exception, with tofu and your favorite fajita veggies all roasted on the same pan. The crisp, golden tofu and blistered peppers are given a nice squeeze of lime juice and sprinkle of cilantro at the end, making it a breeze to scoop and serve in warm tortillas. Serve with your favorite guacamole and vegan sour cream for a hearty and flavorful meal.

1 block (16 ounces, or 455 g) extra-firm tofu
2 tablespoons (30 ml) avocado oil, divided
2 tablespoons (30 ml) tamari
1 packet (1 ounce, or 28 g) fajita seasoning, divided
1 red bell pepper
1 orange bell pepper
1 yellow bell pepper
½ yellow onion

TO SERVE
8 fajita tortillas, warmed
½ lime
Fresh cilantro, chopped
Guacamole
Vegan sour cream

1. Preheat the oven to 425°F (220°C, or gas mark 7).

2. Drain the tofu and wrap it in a few layers of paper towels. Wrap a clean kitchen towel around the paper towels and press out as much water as possible. Change out the paper towels and kitchen towel and continue to press until the tofu is quite dry.

3. Slice the tofu into ½-inch (1.3 cm)-wide pieces about 2 inches (5 cm) long. Place the tofu pieces in a zip top bag or a large container with a tight-fitting lid. Add 1 tablespoon (15 ml) of the avocado oil, the tamari, and half of the fajita seasoning packet (about 1½ tablespoons). Shake the bag or container to coat the tofu. Set the tofu aside while you prep the veggies.

4. Slice the red, orange, and yellow bell peppers into ½-inch (1.3 cm) strips. Thinly slice the yellow onion.

5. Transfer the veggies to a large bowl and drizzle with the remaining tablespoon (15 ml) of avocado oil. Season with the remaining fajita seasoning and stir to coat.

6. Line a large baking sheet with parchment paper. Transfer the veggies and tofu to the baking sheet, making sure all of the ingredients are arranged in a single layer.

7. Roast for 10 minutes, then flip the tofu pieces and gently toss the veggies with tongs. Roast for another 15 minutes, until the peppers are blistered and the tofu is golden and slightly crisp. Squeeze the lime over the veggies and tofu and sprinkle with cilantro.

8. To serve, divide the tofu and fajita veggies between the tortillas. Top with guacamole and vegan sour cream.

BUTTERNUT SQUASH AND SOY CHORIZO TACOS

SERVES 4 I'm a big fan of using soy chorizo in plant-based tacos because there is no chopping or seasoning required. It is reliable and delicious every time, no matter the brand. This recipe is super quick as written, but you can take a shortcut by adding precut butternut squash to your shopping list. Simply roast it on a sheet pan with avocado oil, sea salt, and black pepper, and dinner is served in less than 30 minutes. Fresh cilantro and chopped red onion are the only toppings you need to complete this ultra-flavorful dish.

1 butternut squash, peeled
2 tablespoons (30 ml) avocado oil
1 teaspoon fine sea salt
Freshly cracked black pepper
1 package (12 ounces, or 340 g) soy chorizo

TO SERVE
8 corn tortillas, warmed
Fresh cilantro, chopped
Red onion, finely chopped
2 limes, cut into wedges

1. Preheat the oven to 425°F (220°C, or gas mark 7) and line a baking sheet with parchment paper.

2. Slice the butternut squash in half lengthwise and scoop out the seeds. Dice the squash into ½-inch (1.3 cm) cubes.

3. Transfer the butternut squash cubes to the prepared baking sheet. Drizzle with avocado oil and sprinkle with salt and pepper. Toss to coat.

4. Roast the butternut squash for 20 to 25 minutes, stirring the pieces halfway through. When done, the butternut squash should be golden and fork tender.

5. Meanwhile, squeeze the soy chorizo from the casing directly into a nonstick pan and turn to medium heat. Use a spatula to break up the soy chorizo and cook, stirring occasionally, for 8 to 10 minutes, until heated through and slightly crisp on the edges.

6. To serve, divide the soy chorizo between the tortillas. Top with roasted butternut squash, cilantro, red onion, and a squeeze of lime juice.

KOREAN-STYLE TOFU TACOS

SERVES 4 TO 6 This is my husband's favorite recipe in this book—and it might be mine, too. Asian is my favorite flavor profile, and it was so much fun to experiment with making a bulgogi-inspired plant-based taco. Shredded tofu soaks up so much flavor, and the soft, chewy texture is perfect for tucking into warm tortillas. Kimchi, cucumber, and cilantro offer fresh contrast to the warm, spicy filling. You'll be going back for seconds with this one.

2 blocks (16 ounces, or 455 g each) super-firm tofu
½ cup (120 ml) low-sodium soy sauce
3 tablespoons (45 g) gochujang
2 tablespoons (30 ml) rice vinegar
¼ cup (60 ml) maple syrup
¼ cup (60 ml) toasted sesame oil
1 tablespoon (8 g) ginger, grated
6 garlic cloves, grated

TO SERVE
12 corn tortillas, warmed
1 cup (100 g) vegan kimchi
2 Persian cucumbers, sliced or julienned with a peeler
1 bunch fresh cilantro, chopped

1. Preheat the oven to 400°F (200°C, or gas mark 6) and line a large baking sheet or 2 smaller baking sheets with parchment paper.

2. Drain the tofu and wrap it in a few layers of paper towels. Wrap a clean kitchen towel around the paper towels and press out as much moisture as possible.

3. Using the large hole side on a box grater, shred the tofu into a large mixing bowl.

4. In a separate bowl, whisk together the low-sodium soy sauce, gochujang, rice vinegar, maple syrup, toasted sesame oil, ginger, and garlic.

5. Pour half of the sauce over the shredded tofu and use a silicone spatula to stir until the tofu has fully absorbed the sauce.

6. Spread the tofu in a single layer across the baking sheet(s) and bake for 20 minutes, stirring and flipping the tofu halfway through. When done, it should be lightly browned and crisp on the edges. Remove the tofu from the oven.

7. Warm a large, deep-sided nonstick skillet over medium heat. Add the baked tofu to the skillet, then pour the remaining sauce over top. Cook, stirring occasionally, for 5 to 7 minutes, until the tofu has absorbed most of the sauce and appears dark golden. Turn off the heat.

8. To serve, divide the Korean-style tofu between the tortillas. Top each with vegan kimchi, cucumbers, and cilantro.

SOY CHORIZO TACOS WITH MANGO SALSA

SERVES 5 TO 6 Bookmark this recipe for those hectic Tuesday nights when you only have a few minutes to get dinner on the table. The mango salsa can be made the weekend prior and stored in the fridge for a nearly effortless meal. You can find soy chorizo at most grocery stores near the tofu and other refrigerated plant-based items. Soy chorizo can be spicy, depending on the brand, so use discretion if you're planning to serve this to younger kids or those who are sensitive to heat.

1 tablespoon (30 ml) avocado oil
½ white onion, finely chopped
2 packages (12 ounces, or 340 g each) soy chorizo

TO SERVE
16 corn tortillas, warmed
Mango Salsa (page 29)

1. Warm the avocado oil in a nonstick or stainless steel pan over medium heat. Add the onion and sauté until fragrant and slightly softened, about 3 minutes, stirring frequently.

2. Add the soy chorizo to the pan and break it up with a spatula. Cook the soy chorizo for 7 to 8 minutes, until slightly crispy on the edges and heated through. Turn off the heat.

3. To serve, divide the cooked soy chorizo between the tortillas and top each with a generous spoonful of Mango Salsa.

GREEK GYRO-STYLE TEMPEH TACOS

SERVES 4 Visiting Greece is on my bucket list, but until I make it there, I'll keep eating these delicious Greek-inspired tacos. The base of these tacos is made with crumbled tempeh sautéed in a savory sauce until golden brown and slightly crisp. Steaming the tempeh first helps it absorb more flavor—don't skip this step! Drizzle your taco with vegan tzatziki and finish it off with sliced cucumber, tomato, and red onion.

2 packages (8 ounces, or 225 g each) tempeh, sliced into 1-inch (2.5 cm) pieces
1 tablespoon (15 ml) avocado oil
3 garlic cloves, finely chopped

FOR THE SAUCE
½ cup (120 ml) tamari
1 tablespoon (15 ml) red wine vinegar
1 tablespoon (15 ml) lemon juice
½ tablespoon dried oregano
1 teaspoon cumin
1 teaspoon dried thyme
¼ cup (36 g) coconut sugar
Freshly cracked black pepper

TO SERVE
8 fajita tortillas, warmed
1 pint (284 g) cherry tomatoes, halved
2 Persian cucumber, sliced and quartered
Red onion, thinly sliced
Vegan Tzatziki (page 55)

1. Cover the bottom of a medium nonstick or stainless steel skillet with water and bring it to a simmer. Carefully place the tempeh pieces in the water and cover the skillet. Steam for 10 minutes.

2. Remove the tempeh from the skillet with tongs and set it aside on a cutting board to cool. Wipe the skillet dry and return it to the stove.

3. To make the sauce: In a medium bowl, whisk together the tamari, red wine vinegar, lemon juice, oregano, cumin, thyme, coconut sugar, and pepper. Set aside.

4. When the tempeh is cool enough to handle, use your hands to crumble it into small pieces or finely chop it with a knife.

5. Pour the avocado oil into the skillet and turn the heat to medium-high. When the oil is hot, add the crumbled tempeh and stir. Sauté the tempeh until it turns light golden, about 4 to 5 minutes. Add the garlic to the skillet and sauté for 30 seconds more.

6. Pour the sauce over the tempeh and stir to combine. Continue to sauté, stirring occasionally, for 10 to 12 minutes more, until the sauce has reduced and the tempeh is dark and crispy in some spots. Turn off the heat.

7. To serve, divide the tempeh between the tortillas. Top with cherry tomatoes, Persian cucumber, red onion, and Vegan Tzatziki.

PLANT-POWERED PROTEIN TACOS

TOFU CARNITAS TACOS WITH APPLE SALSA

SERVES 4 Shredding tofu on a box grater is my new favorite way to prepare tofu for tacos. The tiny pieces soak up so much flavor and get a nice chewy texture with crispy edges when pan-fried. Top your tofu carnitas tacos with apple salsa, which strikes the perfect balance of sweet and spicy. I like these tacos served on soft corn tortillas, but the tofu carnitas are also delicious on flour and grain-free varieties.

1 block (16 ounces, or 455 g) super-firm tofu (or extra-firm tofu)

FOR THE MARINADE
1 teaspoon garlic powder
1 teaspoon onion powder
1 tablespoon (8 g) chili powder
½ tablespoon dried oregano
1 teaspoon cumin
¼ cup (60 ml) orange juice
¼ cup (60 ml) avocado oil
1½ teaspoons fine sea salt

FOR THE APPLE SALSA
Juice of 1 lime
1 sweet apple, cored and finely diced
⅓ cup (55 g) finely chopped red onion
½ jalapeño, seeds removed and finely chopped
¼ cup (4 g) finely chopped fresh cilantro
½ teaspoon agave syrup
¼ teaspoon fine sea salt

TO SERVE
8 soft corn tortillas
1 lime, sliced into wedges

1. Drain the tofu and wrap it in a few layers of paper towels. Wrap a clean kitchen towel around the paper towels and press out as much moisture as possible.

2. Using the large hole side on a box grater, shred the tofu into a large skillet.

3. To make the marinade: Combine the garlic powder, onion powder, chili powder, oregano, cumin, orange juice, avocado oil, and salt in a mixing bowl. Whisk to blend.

4. Pour the marinade over the shredded tofu and stir, until the tofu soaks up all of the liquid.

5. Place the tofu in a skillet over medium heat and cook until it is deep golden and crispy on the edges, about 25 to 30 minutes. Stir every 5 minutes or so to ensure it crisps evenly. Turn off the heat.

6. To make the apple salsa: Squeeze the lime juice into a bowl. Add the diced apple to the lime juice and toss frequently to prevent the apple from browning. Add the red onion, jalapeño, cilantro, agave syrup, and salt. Toss to combine.

7. Warm the tortillas in the microwave or carefully toast them one at a time over an open flame on the stove.

8. To serve, spoon the tofu carnitas down the center of each tortilla and top with fresh apple salsa.

COCONUT-CRUSTED TOFU TACOS

SERVES 4 Coating tofu in panko breadcrumbs and shredded coconut imparts a delightfully crunchy bite to these plant protein–packed tacos. First, marinate your tofu to infuse it with savory flavor. A quick dusting of panko and coconut flakes, plus 20 minutes in the oven, is all that stands between you and dinner tonight. Make the pineapple salsa ahead of time for truly breezy meal prep.

1 package (16 ounces, or 455 g) extra-firm tofu
¼ cup (60 ml) soy sauce
¼ cup (60 ml) maple syrup
1 tablespoon (15 ml) lime juice
½ tablespoon fresh ginger, grated
⅓ cup (42 g) all-purpose flour
½ cup (120 ml) water
½ cup (25 g) panko breadcrumbs
¾ cup (60 g) shredded coconut

FOR THE SPICY MAYO SAUCE
½ cup (115 g) vegan mayo
2 teaspoons sriracha
2 teaspoons lime juice
¼ teaspoon fine sea salt

TO SERVE
Shredded cabbage
8 flour tortillas, warmed
Pineapple Salsa (page 106)

1. Preheat the oven to 400°F (200°C, or gas mark 6) and line a large baking sheet with parchment paper.

2. Wrap the tofu in a few layers of paper towels. Wrap a clean kitchen towel around the paper towels and press out as much water as possible.

3. Slice the tofu into ½-inch (1.3 cm) pieces about 2 inches (5 cm) long and press with paper towels again.

4. In a shallow bowl, combine the soy sauce, maple syrup, lime juice, and ginger.

5. Place the tofu pieces in the bowl in a single layer and tilt the bowl back and forth to coat the tofu on all sides. Set the tofu aside to absorb the flavors, flipping the pieces occasionally.

6. Set 2 shallow bowls on the countertop. To the first one, add the flour and water and whisk to combine. In the second one, combine the panko breadcrumbs and shredded coconut.

7. Working one piece at a time, shake excess marinade from the tofu and dip it in the flour mixture, allowing excess to drip back into the bowl. Place the tofu in the panko breadcrumb/coconut mixture and turn to coat it on all sides. Transfer to the baking sheet.

8. Bake the tofu for 20 minutes. Flip each piece over and bake for 10 to 15 minutes more, until the tofu is crisp and deep golden.

9. To make the spicy mayo sauce: Add all of the ingredients to a small bowl and stir to combine.

10. To serve, arrange some shredded cabbage in the center of each tortilla. Add a few pieces of coconut crusted tofu, top with pineapple salsa, and drizzle with spicy mayo sauce.

MAPLE MISO TEMPEH TACOS

SERVES 4 Miso paste is one of my absolute favorite ingredients for adding umami flavor to plant-based proteins. Here, sweet maple syrup balances it out to make a delicious sticky glaze for tempeh. Together with sesame slaw, Pickled Red Onion (page 27), and thinly sliced cucumber, this Asian-inspired taco recipe will add loads of savory flavor and crunchy texture to your Tuesday night meal.

2 packages (8 ounces, or 225 g each) tempeh
2 tablespoons (30 ml) toasted sesame oil

FOR THE SAUCE
¼ cup (60 ml) maple syrup
¼ cup (63 g) miso paste
2 teaspoons low-sodium soy sauce
2 teaspoons toasted sesame oil
1½ teaspoons rice vinegar

FOR THE SESAME SLAW
2 cups (140 g) shredded green cabbage
1 cup (110 g) shredded carrot
1 tablespoon (15 ml) lime juice
½ tablespoon toasted sesame oil
¼ teaspoon fine sea salt

TO SERVE
8 flour tortillas, warmed
Pickled Red Onion (page 27)
1 cucumber, thinly sliced into matchsticks
Toasted sesame seeds

1. Slice the tempeh blocks crosswise into 1-inch (2.5 cm) pieces.

2. Fill a small pan with ½ inch (1.3 cm) of water and bring it to a simmer over medium heat. Place the tempeh pieces in the simmering water and cover the pan. Turn the heat to low and steam the tempeh for 10 minutes.

3. To make the sauce: Combine the maple syrup, miso paste, low-sodium soy sauce, toasted sesame oil, and rice vinegar in a small bowl. Whisk to dissolve the miso paste into the other ingredients. Set aside.

4. Transfer the steamed tempeh to a cutting board. Roughly chop the tempeh into small pieces.

5. Drain the water from the pan and wipe it dry. Return the pan to the stove and place over medium heat. Add the sesame oil.

6. When the oil is hot, transfer the tempeh to the pan and cook for 6 to 8 minutes, stirring occasionally, until crisp and browned in some spots.

7. Pour the maple miso sauce over the tempeh, reserving a few spoonfuls for serving. Allow the tempeh to sit for a few minutes to get crispy before stirring. Cook the tempeh for another 5 to 7 minutes, stirring once or twice, until the tempeh is caramelized and sticky. Turn off the heat.

8. To make the sesame slaw: Combine all of the ingredients in a large bowl and stir to blend.

9. To serve, add some sesame slaw to each tortilla. Top with the maple miso tempeh, Pickled Red Onion, sliced cucumber, and toasted sesame seeds. Drizzle the tacos with a bit more maple miso sauce, if desired.

› **CHAPTER 6** ‹

VEGGIE LOADED TACOS

It's so easy to get stuck in a vegetable rut, especially when veggies make up the bulk of your diet. This chapter is full of ideas for spicing up your dinner routine by preparing and seasoning your favorite vegetables in new and exciting ways. Gochujang Sweet Potato Street Tacos (page 145) use Korean chili paste to add new life to your favorite root veggie. Jerk Plantain Tacos with Mango Salsa (page 129) asks you to think about a plantain, the banana's bigger cousin, as a vegetable (although it's technically a fruit).

The final recipe in this book will, hopefully, change your mind about Brussels sprouts. Chipotle Roasted Brussels Sprout Tacos (page 146) challenge the notion that Brussels sprouts are stinky little cabbage bombs and may actually have you eating them straight off the pan. I hope these veggie loaded tacos reinvigorate your love of vegetables and inspire you to think of new ways to enjoy them inside and outside of a tortilla.

MISO-GLAZED MUSHROOM TACOS

SERVES 4 Miso paste is often used in Japanese cooking, and it lends a funky, rich, umami flavor to soups, marinades, and sauces. You can find it in most supermarkets in the aisle with Asian products and in Asian grocery stores. In this recipe, miso paste is whisked together with soy sauce, maple syrup, garlic, and rice vinegar to create a delicious glaze for tender button mushrooms. Bok choy and quick pickled carrots offer a nice crunch and punch of fresh flavor.

12 ounces (340 g) button mushrooms
1 tablespoon (15 ml) toasted sesame oil
1 teaspoon toasted sesame seeds

FOR THE MISO GLAZE
2 tablespoons (32 g) miso paste
1 tablespoon (15 ml) low-sodium soy sauce
2 tablespoons (30 ml) maple syrup
2 teaspoons rice vinegar
1 garlic clove, grated

FOR THE QUICK PICKLED CARROTS
½ cup (120 ml) hot water
½ cup (120 ml) rice vinegar
2 teaspoons sugar
1 teaspoon fine sea salt
1 large carrot, peeled

TO SERVE
2 baby bok choy, finely shredded
8 flour tortillas, warmed
2 scallions, thinly sliced

1. Bring a pot of water to a boil. Add the whole mushrooms to the boiling water and cover. Reduce the heat slightly and simmer the mushrooms for 15 minutes.

2. To make the miso glaze: Combine the miso paste, low-sodium soy sauce, maple syrup, rice vinegar, and garlic in a small bowl. Whisk with a fork to blend the miso paste into the liquid ingredients.

3. To make the quick pickled carrots: Combine the hot water, rice vinegar, sugar, and salt in a heat-safe bowl. Stir to dissolve the sugar and salt into the liquid, microwaving in 30-second intervals if necessary.

4. Use a sharp vegetable peeler to slice the carrot into thin ribbons. Place the carrot ribbons into the bowl of pickling liquid and press down to submerge all of the carrots. Set aside.

5. When the mushrooms are done boiling, use a slotted spoon to transfer them to a clean kitchen towel and pat them dry.

6. Warm the toasted sesame oil in a nonstick skillet over medium-high heat. When the oil is hot, transfer the mushrooms to the pan. Sauté the mushrooms until browned, about 5 minutes.

7. Pour the miso glaze over the mushrooms and reduce the heat to medium. Continue to sauté, stirring occasionally, until the mushrooms are coated and the glaze has thickened, about 8 minutes more. Sprinkle the toasted sesame seeds over the mushrooms.

8. To serve, divide the shredded bok choy between the tortillas. Top with a few miso glazed mushrooms, pickled carrots, and scallions.

JERK PLANTAIN TACOS WITH MANGO SALSA

SERVES 4   If this is your first time cooking with plantains, you're in for a major treat. Plantains look like giant bananas, but they have thicker skin and a firmer, starchier flesh. For this recipe, select ripe plantains that are yellow with black spots on the skin. They should be somewhat soft, but not mushy. Sliced, tossed in jerk seasoning, and pan fried, these plantains make a delicious and hearty filling for Caribbean-inspired tacos.

2 ripe plantains, peeled
1½ tablespoons (24 g) jerk seasoning
1 tablespoon (9 g) coconut sugar
1 tablespoon (15 ml) avocado oil

FOR THE LIME CREMA
1 cup (128 g) raw cashews
¼ cup (60 ml) water, plus more as needed
Juice of 2 limes
Zest of 1 lime
½ teaspoon fine sea salt

TO SERVE
Shredded romaine lettuce
8 corn tortillas, warmed
Mango Salsa (page 29)

1. Cut the plantains into spears about 3 inches (7.5 cm) long and ½-inch (1.3 cm) wide. Transfer the plantain pieces to a plate.

2. Combine the jerk seasoning and coconut sugar in a small bowl. Sprinkle the spice mixture over the plantains, turning the pieces to coat all sides.

3. Warm the avocado oil in a nonstick skillet over medium heat. When the oil is hot, add the plantains in a single layer. Cook for 3 minutes on each side, until caramelized and nearly blackened. Turn off the heat.

4. To make the lime crema: Combine all of the ingredients in a high-speed blender and blend for 1 to 2 minutes, until very smooth. Add a touch more water to thin as necessary and adjust the lime juice and salt to taste.

5. To serve, add a small handful of shredded romaine lettuce to each tortilla. Top with a few pieces of plantain and a spoonful of Mango Salsa. Drizzle with lime crema.

CRISPY AVOCADO TACOS

SERVES 4   Crunchy on the outside and creamy on the inside, air-fried or baked avocado slices provide a satisfying base for these plant-based tacos. A drizzle of zesty chipotle aioli takes these tacos over the top with subtly spicy flavor. I highly recommend using your air fryer for the crispiest results, but you can use the oven method if necessary. These tacos are best enjoyed right away while still crispy. The Chipotle Aioli (page 26) can be made ahead of time to get dinner on the table fast.

3 avocados (slightly firm, not too ripe)
¼ cup (31 g) all-purpose flour
½ teaspoon garlic powder
½ teaspoon fine sea salt
⅓ cup (80 ml) plain nondairy milk
1 cup (50 g) panko breadcrumbs
Avocado oil spray

TO SERVE
Red cabbage, shredded
Green cabbage, shredded
8 flour tortillas, warmed
Chipotle Aioli (page 26)
Fresh cilantro, finely chopped

1. Slice the avocados in half lengthwise and remove the pits. Peel the skin off the avocados and discard.

2. Cut the avocado halves lengthwise into ½-inch (1.3 cm) slices. You should get 4 to 5 good slices per avocado half.

3. Place 3 small bowls on the countertop. To the first one, add the all-purpose flour, garlic powder, and salt. Use a fork to whisk the ingredients together until well combined. Pour the nondairy milk into the second bowl and add the panko breadcrumbs to the third bowl.

4. Lightly coat the air fryer basket with avocado oil spray. If you're baking the avocado slices instead, preheat the oven to 425°F (220°C, or gas mark 7) and line a baking sheet with parchment paper.

5. Working one piece at a time, coat the avocado slices in the flour mixture. Then dip them in the nondairy milk. Finally, coat the avocado pieces in panko breadcrumbs.

6. Transfer the coated avocado slices to the basket of the air fryer in a single layer, or arrange them on the prepared baking sheet if baking. If you're using an air fryer, you'll need to work in batches to not overcrowd the basket.

7. Lightly coat the avocado slices with avocado oil spray. Air fry at 390°F (200°C) degrees for 8 to 10 minutes, until very crispy and golden in color. If baking, after 15 minutes, flip the avocado pieces over, spray them with avocado oil spray once more, and bake for an additional 10 minutes.

8. To serve, divide the shredded cabbage between the tortillas. Top with the crispy avocado slices, drizzle with Chipotle Aioli, and garnish with cilantro.

BBQ JACKFRUIT TACOS

SERVES 4   The BBQ fans at your dinner table will love the familiar flavors and textures in these plant-based tacos. For this recipe, look for cans of young green jackfruit in water or brine, which can be found in the Asian or international aisle of many grocery stores. Once cooked and shredded, jackfruit provides the perfect vehicle for that classic, irresistible BBQ taste and mouthfeel. Fresh cabbage and corn offer crunchy contrast to the jackfruit filling and make these tacos a rollercoaster for your tastebuds.

2 cans (15 ounces, or 425 g each) young green
   jackfruit in water or brine, drained and rinsed
1 tablespoon (15 ml) avocado oil
½ yellow onion, diced
1 jalapeño, finely chopped
2 garlic cloves, finely chopped
¾ cup (188 g) vegan BBQ sauce
¼ cup (60 ml) water
¾ teaspoon fine sea salt
½ teaspoon chili powder
1 tablespoon (15 ml) orange juice

TO SERVE
8 flour tortillas, warmed
1 cup (210 g) sweet corn kernels, warmed
2 cups (140 g) shredded red cabbage
¼ cup (4 g) chopped fresh cilantro
Vegan sour cream
Lime wedges

1. Cut the jackfruit pieces into ¼ inch (6 mm) slices from the core to the outer edge. You should get 2 or 3 slices from each piece of jackfruit. The core is tough but will soften significantly as it's cooked. Set the prepared jackfruit aside.

2. Warm the avocado oil in a large, deep-sided skillet over medium heat. When the oil is hot, add the onion and sauté until soft and fragrant, about 3 minutes. Add the jalapeño and garlic to the pan and cook for 2 minutes more.

3. Add the jackfruit, BBQ sauce, water, salt, and chili powder to the pan. Bring the mixture to a simmer, then cover and cook for another 5 minutes.

4. Uncover the pan. Use a wooden spatula or a potato masher to break up the jackfruit until the strands have separated and it appears shredded. Stir in the orange juice, then turn off the heat.

5. To serve, divide the BBQ jackfruit between the tortillas. Top with corn, red cabbage, and cilantro. Serve with vegan sour cream and lime wedges on the side.

DELICATA SQUASH TACOS WITH MAPLE TAHINI

SERVES 4 I remember being stunned when I first learned that the skin of delicata squash is edible. No peeling required! In this plant-based taco recipe, delicata squash offers a hearty, seasonal base perfect for topping with fresh pomegranate seeds and parsley. If you're willing to put in a little extra effort, set the squash seeds aside and roast them for a zero-waste crunchy taco topping.

2 delicata squash
2 tablespoons (30 ml) avocado oil
1 teaspoon fine sea salt
¼ teaspoon freshly cracked black pepper

FOR THE DELICATA SQUASH SEEDS
Seeds from 2 delicata squash
2 teaspoons avocado oil
½ teaspoon garlic powder
¼ teaspoon fine sea salt

FOR THE MAPLE TAHINI
¼ cup (60 g) tahini
2 teaspoons tamari
1½ teaspoons maple syrup

TO SERVE
12 corn tortillas, warmed
¾ cup (105 g) pomegranate seeds
½ cup (30 g) finely chopped fresh parsley

1. Preheat the oven to 425°F (220°C, or gas mark 7).

2. Slice the delicata squash in half lengthwise and scoop out the seeds. Set the seeds aside in a bowl.

3. Cut the squash halves into ½-inch (1.3 cm) half-moons. Transfer the squash to a large baking sheet lined with parchment paper.

4. Drizzle the squash pieces with avocado oil and sprinkle with salt and pepper. Toss to coat. Roast for 25 minutes, flipping the squash pieces halfway through.

5. To make the roasted delicata squash seeds: Rinse the seeds in a mesh strainer and pick out any pieces of squash membrane that are stuck on.

6. Transfer the rinsed squash seeds to a clean kitchen towel and pat them dry.

7. Line another baking sheet with parchment paper. Scatter the squash seeds on the baking sheet and drizzle with avocado oil. Sprinkle with garlic powder and salt and toss to coat.

8. When the squash is done, remove it from the oven and lower the temperature to 350°F (170°C, or gas mark 3). Roast the seeds for 20 minutes, stirring them halfway through, until golden and crisp. Tip: Return the delicata squash to the oven to briefly warm it just before serving.

9. To make the maple tahini: Pour all of the ingredients into a small bowl and whisk to combine. Add more tamari or maple syrup to taste.

10. To serve, spread a thin layer of maple tahini on the tortillas. Top each with roasted delicata squash, pomegranate seeds, parsley, and roasted delicata squash seeds.

SMOKY BUTTERNUT SQUASH AND APPLE TACOS

SERVES 4   I find it so fun to experiment with unexpected flavor and texture pairings within the familiar format of a taco. This butternut squash taco recipe leans on crisp apple slices for crunch and a burst of sweet, juicy flavor. You can use any type of apple, but I like Honeycrisp and Gala best in this recipe. Raw pepitas are small, green ovals that are incredibly delicious when roasted with a little bit of oil and sea salt.

1 butternut squash, peeled
2 tablespoons (30 ml) avocado oil
1 teaspoon fine sea salt
1 teaspoon smoked paprika
Freshly cracked black pepper

FOR THE ROASTED PEPITAS
1 cup (136 g) raw pepitas
1 teaspoon avocado oil
½ teaspoon fine sea salt

TO SERVE
1 apple, thinly sliced (Honeycrisp or Gala preferred)
8 corn tortillas, warmed
Chipotle Aioli (page 26)

1. Preheat the oven to 425°F (220°C, or gas mark 7) and line a large baking sheet with parchment paper.

2. Slice the butternut squash in half lengthwise and scoop out the seeds. Slice the butternut squash into ¼-inch (6 mm) wedges. Transfer to a large mixing bowl.

3. Drizzle the butternut squash with avocado oil and season with salt, smoked paprika, and pepper. Toss to coat.

4. Transfer the squash to the prepared baking sheet and arrange them in a single layer, taking care not to overlap if possible.

5. Roast the butternut squash for 20 to 25 minutes, flipping the pieces halfway through. When done, the butternut squash should be golden and fork tender. Remove from the oven, but leave it on.

6. To make the roasted pepitas: Combine the raw pepitas, avocado oil, and salt in a mixing bowl and toss to coat.

7. Line another baking sheet with parchment paper. Pour the pepitas onto the baking sheet and arrange them in a single layer. Roast the pepitas for 20 minutes, stirring them halfway through. Keep an eye on the pepitas in the last couple minutes of roasting so they don't get too scorched.

8. To serve, divide the squash and apple slices between the tortillas. Drizzle each with Chipotle Aioli and sprinkle with roasted pepitas.

VEGGIE LOADED TACOS

MUSHROOM BÁNH MÌ-STYLE TACOS

SERVES 2 TO 3 Bánh mì is a Vietnamese sandwich served on a baguette with a crunchy outside and pillowy soft inside. This is my plant-based spin on bánh mì, all wrapped up in a flour tortilla. A quick sriracha mayo along with fresh herbs, radishes, and jalapeño slices bring a nice brightness to these tacos inspired by traditional Vietnamese cuisine.

FOR THE MUSHROOMS
12 ounces (340 g) king oyster mushrooms
1 tablespoon (15 ml) avocado oil

FOR THE SAUCE
¼ cup (60 ml) tamari
1½ tablespoons (25 ml) lime juice
¼ cup (60 ml) maple syrup
½ teaspoon garlic powder
6 scallions, white and light green parts, finely chopped

FOR THE PICKLED CARROTS
1 cup (235 ml) water
1 tablespoon (13 g) sugar
½ teaspoon fine sea salt
½ cup (120 ml) rice vinegar
2 carrots, very thinly sliced into ⅛-inch (3 mm) matchsticks

FOR THE SRIRACHA MAYO
½ cup (115 g) vegan mayo
1½ tablespoons (25 ml) sriracha

TO SERVE
6 taco-size flour tortillas, warmed
4 radishes, thinly sliced
1 bunch fresh cilantro leaves
1 bunch fresh mint leaves
1 jalapeño, thinly sliced (optional)

1. Rake a fork through the stems of the king oyster mushrooms until they are finely shredded. Thinly slice the mushroom caps with a sharp knife.

2. Heat the avocado oil in a large nonstick skillet over medium heat. When the oil is hot, add the prepared king oyster mushrooms. Sauté the mushrooms for 5 to 6 minutes, stirring occasionally, until the mushrooms have cooked down slightly and most of the water has evaporated.

3. To make the sauce: Combine the tamari, lime juice, maple syrup, garlic powder, and scallions in a small bowl. Whisk with a fork to blend the ingredients.

4. Pour the sauce over the mushrooms and stir to coat. Reduce the heat slightly to maintain a gentle simmer for 15 to 20 minutes, until the mushrooms are tender and golden brown and the sauce is thick and slightly sticky. Turn off the heat.

5. To make the pickled carrots: Bring water to a boil in a medium saucepan. Turn off the heat, then add the sugar and salt. Stir until dissolved.

6. Pour the rice vinegar into the saucepan, then add the sliced carrots. Use a spatula to push the carrots down so that all of the pieces are submerged. Allow the carrots to sit in the pickling liquid for at least 2 hours.

7. To make the sriracha mayo: Combine the vegan mayo and the sriracha in a small bowl. Stir to combine.

8. To serve, use tongs to divide the cooked mushrooms between the tortillas. Top each taco with sliced radish, cilantro, mint, and jalapeño (if using). Drizzle with the sriracha mayo.

JACKFRUIT CARNITAS TOSTADAS

SERVES 4 Making jackfruit carnitas is all about having a fully stocked spice rack. A few pantry and fridge items, along with fresh orange and lime, are all you need to make incredibly delicious tostadas that offer a satisfying crunch and mouthwatering flavor. To speed up dinner prep, make the Salsa Verde (page 21) over the weekend and store it in the fridge until dinnertime.

2 cans (14 ounces, or 395 g each) young green jackfruit in water or brine
1 tablespoon (15 ml) avocado oil
½ cup (80 g) diced white onion
2 garlic cloves, finely chopped

FOR THE SAUCE
1 teaspoon garlic powder
1 teaspoon onion powder
1 tablespoon (8 g) chili powder
¼ teaspoon ground cloves
½ tablespoon dried oregano
1 teaspoon cumin
Freshly cracked black pepper
½ teaspoon fine sea salt
¼ cup (60 ml) orange juice
2 tablespoons (30 ml) lime juice
2 tablespoons (30 ml) tamari
1 tablespoon (15 ml) maple syrup
½ cup (120 ml) water

TO SERVE
8 Tostada Shells (page 18)
Salsa Verde (page 21)
White onion, finely chopped
Fresh cilantro, finely chopped

1. Drain the liquid from the cans of jackfruit and rinse the pieces thoroughly. Set aside.

2. To make the sauce: In a medium bowl, whisk together the garlic powder, onion powder, chili powder, ground cloves, dried oregano, cumin, pepper, salt, orange juice, lime juice, tamari, maple syrup, and water. Set aside.

3. Warm the avocado oil in a large skillet over medium heat. Add the onion and sauté until softened, about 5 minutes. Add the garlic to the skillet and sauté 2 minutes more.

4. Transfer the jackfruit and sauce to the skillet and bring to a boil. Reduce the heat to medium-low and cover. Simmer the jackfruit for 45 minutes, until very tender. Turn off the heat and shred the jackfruit with 2 forks.

5. Preheat the oven to 400°F (200°C, or gas mark 6) and line a large baking sheet with parchment paper.

6. Scoop the shredded jackfruit onto the baking sheet and spread it in an even layer. Lightly coat the jackfruit with avocado oil spray. Roast the jackfruit for 25 minutes, stirring halfway through, until browned and slightly crisp on the edges.

7. To serve, divide the jackfruit carnitas between the tostada shells. Drizzle with Salsa Verde and garnish with chopped onion and cilantro.

VEGGIE LOADED TACOS

ROASTED PORTOBELLO MUSHROOM TACOS

....

SERVES 4   I must admit that I've never been a big por-tobello mushroom fan. That is, until I stepped outside of my comfort zone and made this recipe. I wanted a hearty taco that would allow a drizzle of zesty Chimich-urri (page 68) to shine. Here, portobello mushrooms are marinated and roasted, sliced thin, and layered in warm tortillas with arugula, cherry tomatoes, avocado, and Pickled Red Onion (page 27).

3 garlic cloves, grated
1 teaspoon paprika
1½ teaspoons cumin
¼ cup (60 ml) low-sodium soy sauce
2 tablespoons (30 ml) balsamic vinegar
1 tablespoon (15 ml) avocado oil
4 large portobello mushroom caps, wiped clean

TO SERVE
6 ounces (170 g) arugula
8 corn or flour tortillas, warmed
Cherry tomatoes, quartered
2 avocados, peeled and sliced
Pickled Red Onion (page 27)
Chimichurri (page 68)

1. Preheat the oven to 400°F (200°C, or gas mark 6) and line a large baking sheet with aluminum foil.

2. In a large zip top bag or shallow baking dish, combine the garlic, paprika, cumin, low-sodium soy sauce, vinegar, and avocado oil.

3. Place the portobello mushroom caps in the zip top bag or baking dish and toss to coat. Allow the mush-rooms to marinate for 10 minutes.

4. Place the portobello mushroom caps stem-side up on the baking sheet. Roast for 15 minutes, then flip the mushrooms and roast for 5 minutes more. When done, the mushrooms should be very tender, deep brown, and fragrant.

5. Transfer the mushrooms to a cutting board and slice them into ½-inch (1.3 cm) wide strips.

6. To serve, add a small handful of arugula to each tortilla. Top with sliced mushroom, cherry tomato, avo-cado, and Pickled Red Onion. Drizzle with Chimichurri.

GOCHUJANG SWEET POTATO STREET TACOS

SERVES 4 If you are new to gochujang, this recipe is a great introduction. Gochujang is a fermented chili paste used in Korean cooking to add spicy, umami flavor to proteins and vegetables. Whisk it together with maple syrup and low-sodium soy sauce to create a sticky glaze for roasted sweet potatoes in this delicious taco recipe. Refreshing quick pickled cucumbers, scallions, and cilantro keep the flavors in balance.

2 tablespoons (30 ml) avocado oil
¼ cup (60 g) gochujang paste
2 tablespoons (30 ml) maple syrup
2 tablespoons (30 ml) low-sodium soy sauce
1½ pounds (680 g) sweet potatoes, sliced into ½-inch (1.3 cm) pieces

FOR QUICK PICKLED CUCUMBERS
¼ cup (60 ml) rice vinegar
2 tablespoons (30 ml) toasted sesame oil
1 teaspoon sugar
1 teaspoon fine sea salt
2 Persian cucumbers, thinly sliced

TO SERVE
12 street taco–size flour tortillas, warmed
Scallions, thinly sliced
Fresh cilantro, finely chopped
Toasted sesame seeds

1. Preheat the oven to 425°F (220°C, or gas mark 7) and line a large baking sheet with parchment paper.

2. In a large mixing bowl combine the avocado oil, gochujang paste, maple syrup, and low-sodium soy sauce.

3. Transfer the sweet potato pieces to the bowl and toss to coat.

4. Leaving excess sauce behind in the bowl, spread the sweet potato pieces in a single layer on the prepared baking sheet. Roast for 25 minutes, flipping halfway through. When done, the sweet potato pieces should be tender and sticky. Drizzle with any sauce leftover in the bowl.

5. To make the quick pickled cucumbers: Combine the rice vinegar, toasted sesame oil, sugar, and salt in a heat-safe bowl. Microwave for 15 seconds, then stir to dissolve the sugar and salt.

6. Add the sliced cucumber to the pickling liquid and transfer the bowl to the refrigerator. Stir the cucumbers occasionally.

7. To serve, add a few pieces of roasted sweet potato to each tortilla. Top with pickled cucumbers, scallions, cilantro, and toasted sesame seeds.

CHIPOTLE ROASTED BRUSSELS SPROUT TACOS

SERVES 4   If you're imagining stinky steamed Brussels sprouts you were forced to eat as a kid, let me stop you right there. In this recipe, roasted Brussels sprouts steal the show with a perfectly crisp exterior and tender bite. They are tossed in a smoky chipotle sauce and stuffed into warm corn tortillas with vegan sour cream, Pickled Red Onion (page 27), and fresh cilantro. They will forever change your mind about Brussels sprouts.

1 pound (455 g) Brussels sprouts, halved
1½ tablespoons (25 ml) avocado oil
½ teaspoon fine sea salt
1½ cups (231 g) fresh corn kernels
Zest of 1 lime

FOR THE CHIPOTLE SAUCE
4 garlic cloves, finely chopped
1 tablespoon (15 ml) balsamic vinegar
2 chipotle peppers in adobo sauce
2 tablespoons (30 ml) maple syrup
1 teaspoon chili powder
½ teaspoon fine sea salt

TO SERVE
8 corn tortillas, warmed
Vegan sour cream
Pickled Red Onion (page 27)
Fresh cilantro, finely chopped

1. Preheat the oven to 400°F (200°C, or gas mark 6) and line a large baking sheet with parchment paper.

2. Place the halved Brussels sprouts in a large mixing bowl and toss with avocado oil and ½ teaspoon salt. It's okay if a few of the leaves come loose.

3. Transfer the Brussels sprouts to the prepared baking sheet and place cut-side down in a single layer. Use 2 baking sheets if needed to avoid crowding.

4. Roast the Brussels sprouts for 25 to 30 minutes, flipping them halfway through. When done, the Brussels sprouts should be tender and blackened in some spots.

5. To make the chipotle sauce: To a small blender, add the garlic, vinegar, chipotle peppers, maple syrup, chili powder, and ½ teaspoon salt. Blend until smooth.

6. When the Brussels sprouts are done, transfer them back to the large mixing bowl. Pour half of the chipotle sauce over the Brussels sprouts and stir to coat. Add more sauce for more flavor if desired (you probably won't use all of the sauce).

7. Heat a cast iron skillet over medium-high heat. When the skillet is hot, add the corn kernels and spread them out in an even layer. Allow the corn to blacken a bit on one side before stirring. Continue to cook until the corn is golden and nicely charred. Turn off the heat and stir in the lime zest and a pinch of salt.

8. To serve, divide the roasted Brussels sprouts between the tortillas. Top with the corn, vegan sour cream, Pickled Red Onion, and cilantro.

ACKNOWLEDGMENTS

Creating this cookbook would not have been possible on my own. I have to start by thanking my husband, Andrew. Your unwavering love and support from concept to completion of this project kept me motivated in the most challenging moments. Thank you for taking on more than your fair share of parenting duties so I could test, photograph, and edit recipes. All of those late nights and weekends would have been impossible without you.

Thank you to my daughter, June. You are such an adventurous eater and are always excited to taste mom's new recipes. I'm constantly surprised by how open you are to new flavors and textures. Your curiosity and enthusiasm for food is inspiring. I can't wait for you to discover this cookbook when you're all grown up and learning your way around the kitchen.

To my parents, Dave and Carole. Thank you for making family dinners a priority. Sitting around the kitchen table every night are some of my favorite childhood memories, ones I look forward to continuing with my own family. The vegan tacos on my table look a little different than the food we grew up eating, but the love and intention behind sharing a home-cooked meal is something I will always carry with me.

Thank you to Dan Rosenberg at Harvard Common Press. I appreciate you trusting me with this ambitious concept, and I'm grateful for your support every step of the way. Finally, thank you to Heather Godin for guiding me through the photography and design elements of *The Taco Tuesday Cookbook: Plant-Based*. I feel incredibly fortunate to work with such a fantastic team.

ABOUT THE AUTHOR

Kate Kasbee is a three-time cookbook author, recipe developer, and food photographer. Her approach to cooking celebrates fresh fruits and vegetables, whole grains, and lots of pasta. When she's not writing cookbooks, Kate works at a social media agency creating mouthwatering food video and photo content for national brands. Kate lives in Los Angeles with her husband, their daughter, and a spunky Pug/Boston Terrier mix, Rex.

INDEX

A

agave
- Apple Salsa, 118
- introduction to, 12
- Salsa Verde, 21

ancho chiles: Salsa Roja, 23

apples
- Apple Salsa, 118
- Smoky Butternut Squash and Apple Tacos, 137

arugula
- Crispy Baked Falafel Tacos, 63
- Roasted Portobello Mushroom Tacos, 142

avocado oil
- Baja Tofu Tacos with Citrus Crema, 100–102
- BBQ Jackfruit Tacos, 133
- BBQ Lentil Tacos, 56
- Blackened Cauliflower Tacos with Chipotle Aioli, 76
- Butternut Squash and Soy Chorizo Tacos, 110
- Cauliflower Walnut Tacos, 91
- Cheesy and Crunchy Vegan Gorditas, 46
- Cheesy Bean and Rice Taquitos, 49
- Cheesy Potato Tacos, 45
- Cheesy Smashburger Tacos, 37
- Chile Relleno–Style Tacos, 38
- Chimichurri Grilled Veggie and White Bean Tacos, 68
- Chipotle Roasted Brussels Sprout Tacos, 146
- Crispy Black Bean and Cashew Queso Tacos, 34
- Crispy Chickpea Tacos with Vegan Caesar Dressing, 52
- Crispy Sheet Pan Tacos with Pinto Beans, 59
- Curried Potato and Cauliflower Tacos, 80
- Delicata Squash Seeds, 134
- Delicata Squash Tacos with Maple Tahini, 134
- Flour Tortillas, 19
- Gochujang Sweet Potato Street Tacos, 145
- Greek Gyro-Style Tempeh Tacos, 117
- Grilled Tofu and Pineapple Tacos, 103–105
- Hard Taco Shells, 18
- Harissa Roasted Cauliflower and Chickpea Tacos, 67
- introduction to, 10

- Jackfruit Carnitas Tostadas, 141
- Jalapeño Popper Taquitos, 41
- Jerk Plantain Tacos with Mango Salsa, 129
- Loaded Tater Tot Tacos, 42
- Mexican-Style Street Corn Tacos, 79
- Mushroom Bánh Mì–Style Tacos, 138
- Pinto Bean and Avocado Corn Salsa Tostadas, 71
- Roasted Corn and Poblano Tacos, 83
- Roasted Pepitas, 137
- Roasted Portobello Mushroom Tacos, 142
- Salsa Roja, 23
- Salsa Verde, 21
- Sheet Pan Tofu and Fajita Veggie Tacos, 109
- Smoky Butternut Squash and Apple Tacos, 137
- Smoky Lentil Tacos with Avocado, 72
- Soy Chorizo Tacos with Mango Salsa, 114
- Spicy Peanut Sweet Potato Tacos, 95
- Spicy Plantain and Black Bean Tacos, 64
- Spicy Potato Tacos, 87
- Sweet Potato and Black Bean Tostadas, 60
- Teriyaki Tempeh Tacos with Pineapple Salsa, 106
- Tofu Carnitas Tacos with Apple Salsa, 118
- Tostada Shells, 18

avocados
- Avocado Corn Salsa, 71
- Avocado Mash, 59
- Crispy Avocado Tacos, 130
- Guacamole, 20
- Loaded Tater Tot Tacos, 42
- Roasted Corn and Poblano Tacos, 83
- Roasted Portobello Mushroom Tacos, 142
- Salsa Verde, 21
- Smoky Lentil Tacos with Avocado, 72
- Spicy Potato Tacos, 87
- Sweet Potato and Black Bean Tostadas, 60
- Vegan Caesar Dressing, 52

B

Baja Tofu Tacos with Citrus Crema, 100–102

balsamic vinegar
- Chipotle Roasted Brussels Sprout Tacos, 146
- Roasted Portobello Mushroom Tacos, 142

Bang Bang Cauliflower Tacos, 88

Bang Bang Sauce, 88

BBQ sauce (vegan)
- BBQ Jackfruit Tacos, 133
- BBQ Lentil Tacos, 56
- Crispy BBQ Cauliflower Tacos, 92

beans
- Crispy Black Bean and Cashew Queso Tacos, 34
- introduction to, 12
- Loaded Tater Tot Tacos, 42
- Spicy Plantain and Black Bean Tacos, 64
- Spicy Potato Tacos, 87
- Sweet Potato and Black Bean Tostadas, 60

bell peppers
- Cheesy Bean and Rice Taquitos, 49
- Chimichurri Grilled Veggie and White Bean Tacos, 68
- Mango Salsa, 29
- Mexican-Style Street Corn Tacos, 79
- Sheet Pan Tofu and Fajita Veggie Tacos, 109

black beans
- Crispy Black Bean and Cashew Queso Tacos, 34
- introduction to, 12
- Loaded Tater Tot Tacos, 42
- Spicy Plantain and Black Bean Tacos, 64
- Spicy Potato Tacos, 87
- Sweet Potato and Black Bean Tostadas, 60

Blackened Cauliflower Tacos with Chipotle Aioli, 76

bok choy: Miso-Glazed Mushroom Tacos, 126

broccoli: Jalapeño Popper Taquitos, 41

Brussels sprouts: Chipotle Roasted Brussels Sprout Tacos, 146

Buffalo Cauliflower Tacos with Jalapeño Ranch, 84

butternut squash
- Butternut Squash and Soy Chorizo Tacos, 110
- Smoky Butternut Squash and Apple Tacos, 137

button mushrooms: Miso-Glazed Mushroom Tacos, 126

C

cabbage
- Bang Bang Cauliflower Tacos, 88
- Baja Tofu Tacos with Citrus Crema, 100–102
- BBQ Jackfruit Tacos, 133

|| **153**

Blackened Cauliflower Tacos
with Chipotle Aioli, 76
Buffalo Cauliflower Tacos with
Jalapeño Ranch, 84
Cilantro Lime Slaw, 80
Coconut-Crusted Tofu Tacos, 121
Crispy Avocado Tacos, 130
Grilled Tofu and Pineapple Tacos, 103–105
Sesame Slaw, 122
Spicy Peanut Sauce, 95
cannellini beans
Chimichurri Grilled Veggie and
White Bean Tacos, 68
introduction to, 12
capers: Vegan Caesar Dressing, 52
carrots
Blackened Cauliflower Tacos with
Chipotle Aioli, 76
Buffalo Cauliflower Tacos with
Jalapeño Ranch, 84
Cashew Queso, 24
Mushroom Bánh Mì–Style Tacos, 138
Pickled Carrots, 138
Quick Pickled Carrots, 126
Sesame Slaw, 122
cashews
Cashew Queso, 24
Jalapeño Ranch, 30
Jerk Plantain Tacos with Mango Salsa, 129
cauliflower
Bang Bang Cauliflower Tacos, 88
Blackened Cauliflower Tacos with
Chipotle Aioli, 76
Buffalo Cauliflower Tacos with
Jalapeño Ranch, 84
Cauliflower Walnut Tacos, 91
Crispy BBQ Cauliflower Tacos, 92
Curried Potato and Cauliflower Tacos, 80
Harissa Roasted Cauliflower and Chickpea
Tacos, 67
Sticky Sesame Ginger
Cauliflower Tacos, 96
cayenne
Pinto Bean and Avocado Corn
Salsa Tostadas, 71
Spicy Plantain and Black Bean Tacos, 64
cheddar cheese (vegan)
Cheesy and Crunchy Vegan Gorditas, 46
Cheesy Bean and Rice Taquitos, 49
Cheesy Potato Tacos, 45
Jalapeño Popper Taquitos, 41
Cheesy and Crunchy Vegan Gorditas, 46
Cheesy Bean and Rice Taquitos, 49

Cheesy Potato Tacos, 45
Cheesy Smashburger Tacos, 37
cherry tomatoes
Greek Gyro-Style Tempeh Tacos, 117
Roasted Portobello Mushroom Tacos, 142
Vegan Tzatziki, 55
chickpeas
Crispy Baked Falafel Tacos, 63
Crispy Chickpea Tacos with
Vegan Caesar Dressing, 52
Harissa Roasted Cauliflower and
Chickpea Tacos, 67
introduction to, 12
Mediterranean Chickpea Tacos, 55
Chile Relleno–Style Tacos, 38
chili powder
Baja Tofu Tacos with Citrus Crema,
100–102
BBQ Jackfruit Tacos, 133
BBQ Lentil Tacos, 56
Cashew Queso, 24
Chile Relleno–Style Tacos, 38
Chipotle Roasted Brussels
Sprout Tacos, 146
Jackfruit Carnitas Tostadas, 141
Mexican-Style Street Corn Tacos, 79
Roasted Corn and Poblano Tacos, 83
Smoky Lentil Tacos with Avocado, 72
Spicy Plantain and Black Bean Tacos, 64
Spicy Potato Tacos, 87
Sweet Potato and Black Bean Tostadas, 60
Tofu Carnitas Tacos with Apple Salsa, 118
chili sauce: Bang Bang Sauce, 88
Chimichurri Grilled Veggie and
White Bean Tacos, 68
Chipotle Aioli
Blackened Cauliflower Tacos with
Chipotle Aioli, 76
Crispy Avocado Tacos, 130
recipe, 26
Smoky Butternut Squash and
Apple Tacos, 137
Spicy Potato Tacos, 87
chipotle chili powder: Roasted Corn and
Poblano Tacos, 83
chipotle peppers in adobo sauce
Cauliflower Walnut Tacos, 91
Cheesy Bean and Rice Taquitos, 49
Chipotle Aioli, 26
Chipotle Ranch, 41
Chipotle Roasted Brussels
Sprout Tacos, 146
Smoky Lentil Tacos with Avocado, 72

cilantro
Apple Salsa, 118
Avocado Corn Salsa, 71
Baja Tofu Tacos with Citrus Crema,
100–102
BBQ Jackfruit Tacos, 133
Blackened Cauliflower Tacos with
Chipotle Aioli, 76
Buffalo Cauliflower Tacos with
Jalapeño Ranch, 84
Butternut Squash and Soy
Chorizo Tacos, 110
Cheesy Bean and Rice Taquitos, 49
Cheesy Potato Tacos, 45
Chile Relleno–Style Tacos, 38
Chipotle Ranch, 41
Chipotle Roasted Brussels
Sprout Tacos, 146
Cilantro Lime Slaw, 80
Crispy Avocado Tacos, 130
Crispy Baked Falafel Tacos, 63
Gochujang Sweet Potato Street Tacos, 145
Grilled Tofu and Pineapple Tacos, 103–105
Guacamole, 20
Jackfruit Carnitas Tostadas, 141
Jalapeño Ranch, 30
Korean-Style Tofu Tacos, 113
Loaded Tater Tot Tacos, 42
Mango Salsa, 29
Mexican-Style Street Corn Tacos, 79
Mushroom Bánh Mì–Style Tacos, 138
Pineapple Salsa, 106
Roasted Corn and Poblano Tacos, 83
Salsa Roja, 23
Salsa Verde, 21
Sheet Pan Tofu and Fajita
Veggie Tacos, 109
Spicy Peanut Sauce, 95
Spicy Plantain and Black Bean Tacos, 64
Spicy Potato Tacos, 87
Sweet Potato and Black Bean Tostadas, 60
Citrus Crema, 100–102
Coconut-Crusted Tofu Tacos, 121
coconut sugar
Greek Gyro-Style Tempeh Tacos, 117
Jerk Plantain Tacos with Mango Salsa, 129
Spicy Plantain and Black Bean Tacos, 64
Teriyaki Tempeh Tacos with
Pineapple Salsa, 106
coleslaw
BBQ Lentil Tacos, 56
Cilantro Lime Slaw, 80
Sesame Slaw, 122

corn
Avocado Corn Salsa, 71
BBQ Jackfruit Tacos, 133
Chimichurri Grilled Veggie and
White Bean Tacos, 68
Chipotle Roasted Brussels
Sprout Tacos, 146
Loaded Tater Tot Tacos, 42
Mexican-Style Street Corn Tacos, 79
Roasted Corn and Poblano Tacos, 83
Corn Tortillas
Baja Tofu Tacos with Citrus Crema,
100–102
Bang Bang Cauliflower Tacos, 88
Buffalo Cauliflower Tacos with
Jalapeño Ranch, 84
Butternut Squash and Soy
Chorizo Tacos, 110
Cauliflower Walnut Tacos, 91
Cheesy Potato Tacos, 45
Chile Relleno–Style Tacos, 38
Chipotle Roasted Brussels
Sprout Tacos, 146
Cilantro Lime Slaw, 80
Crispy BBQ Cauliflower Tacos, 92
Delicata Squash Tacos with
Maple Tahini, 134
Grilled Tofu and Pineapple Tacos, 103–105
Hard Taco Shells, 18
introduction to, 12
Jalapeño Popper Taquitos, 41
Jerk Plantain Tacos with Mango Salsa, 129
Korean-Style Tofu Tacos, 113
recipe, 16
Roasted Portobello Mushroom Tacos, 142
Smoky Butternut Squash and
Apple Tacos, 137
Smoky Lentil Tacos with Avocado, 72
Soy Chorizo Tacos with Mango Salsa, 114
Spicy Plantain and Black Bean Tacos, 64
Tofu Carnitas Tacos with Apple Salsa, 118
Tostada Shells, 18
cream cheese (vegan): Jalapeño
Popper Taquitos, 41
Crispy Avocado Tacos, 130
Crispy Baked Falafel Tacos, 63
Crispy BBQ Cauliflower Tacos, 92
Crispy Black Bean and Cashew
Queso Tacos, 34
Crispy Chickpea Tacos with Vegan
Caesar Dressing, 52
crispy onions
Cheesy Smashburger Tacos, 37
Crispy Baked Falafel Tacos, 63

Crispy BBQ Cauliflower Tacos, 92
Vegan Burger Sauce, 37
Crispy Sheet Pan Tacos with Pinto Beans, 59
cucumbers
Crispy Baked Falafel Tacos, 63
Gochujang Sweet Potato Street Tacos, 145
Greek Gyro-Style Tempeh Tacos, 117
Harissa Roasted Cauliflower and
Chickpea Tacos, 67
Korean-Style Tofu Tacos, 113
Maple Miso Tempeh Tacos, 122
Mediterranean Chickpea Tacos, 55
Quick Pickled Cucumbers, 145
cumin
Baja Tofu Tacos with Citrus Crema,
100–102
Chile Relleno–Style Tacos, 38
Crispy Baked Falafel Tacos, 63
Greek Gyro-Style Tempeh Tacos, 117
Grilled Tofu and Pineapple Tacos, 103–105
Jackfruit Carnitas Tostadas, 141
Pinto Bean and Avocado Corn
Salsa Tostadas, 71
Roasted Corn and Poblano Tacos, 83
Roasted Portobello Mushroom Tacos, 142
Smoky Lentil Tacos with Avocado, 72
Spicy Plantain and Black Bean Tacos, 64
Tofu Carnitas Tacos with Apple Salsa, 118
Curried Potato and Cauliflower Tacos, 80

D

delicata squash
Delicata Squash Seeds, 134
Delicata Squash Tacos with
Maple Tahini, 134
Dijon mustard
Cashew Queso, 24
Vegan Caesar Dressing, 52

F

fajita tortillas
Crispy Baked Falafel Tacos, 63
Greek Gyro-Style Tempeh Tacos, 117
Sheet Pan Tofu and Fajita
Veggie Tacos, 109
feta (vegan)
Mediterranean Chickpea Tacos, 55
Mexican-Style Street Corn Tacos, 79
Flour Tortillas
Baja Tofu Tacos with Citrus Crema,
100–102
BBQ Jackfruit Tacos, 133
BBQ Lentil Tacos, 56

Blackened Cauliflower Tacos with
Chipotle Aioli, 76
Buffalo Cauliflower Tacos with
Jalapeño Ranch, 84
Cheesy Bean and Rice Taquitos, 49
Cheesy Smashburger Tacos, 37
Chimichurri Grilled Veggie and
White Bean Tacos, 68
Coconut-Crusted Tofu Tacos, 121
Crispy Avocado Tacos, 130
Crispy Black Bean and Cashew
Queso Tacos, 34
Crispy Sheet Pan Tacos with
Pinto Beans, 59
Gochujang Sweet Potato Street Tacos, 145
Harissa Roasted Cauliflower and
Chickpea Tacos, 67
introduction to, 12
Loaded Tater Tot Tacos, 42
Maple Miso Tempeh Tacos, 122
Mexican-Style Street Corn Tacos, 79
Miso-Glazed Mushroom Tacos, 126
Mushroom Bánh Mì–Style Tacos, 138
Pineapple Salsa, 106
recipe, 19
Roasted Corn and Poblano Tacos, 83
Roasted Portobello Mushroom Tacos, 142
Spicy Peanut Sauce, 95
Spicy Potato Tacos, 87
Sticky Sesame Ginger Cauliflower
Tacos, 96
Vegan Caesar Dressing, 52
fried onions
Cheesy Smashburger Tacos, 37
Crispy Baked Falafel Tacos, 63
Crispy BBQ Cauliflower Tacos, 92
Vegan Burger Sauce, 37

G

garlic
BBQ Jackfruit Tacos, 133
BBQ Lentil Tacos, 56
Cashew Queso, 24
Cheesy Bean and Rice Taquitos, 49
Chile Relleno–Style Tacos, 38
Chimichurri Grilled Veggie and
White Bean Tacos, 68
Chipotle Roasted Brussels
Sprout Tacos, 146
Cilantro Lime Slaw, 80
Crispy Baked Falafel Tacos, 63
Crispy Sheet Pan Tacos with
Pinto Beans, 59
Greek Gyro-Style Tempeh Tacos, 117

INDEX 155

Guacamole, 20
Jackfruit Carnitas Tostadas, 141
Jalapeño Ranch, 30
Korean-Style Tofu Tacos, 113
Lemon Garlic Tahini Sauce, 67
Miso-Glazed Mushroom Tacos, 126
Pinto Bean and Avocado Corn
  Salsa Tostadas, 71
Roasted Portobello Mushroom Tacos, 142
Salsa Roja, 23
Salsa Verde, 21
Sesame Ginger Sauce, 96
Smoky Lentil Tacos with Avocado, 72
Spicy Peanut Sauce, 95
Spicy Plantain and Black Bean Tacos, 64
Teriyaki Tempeh Tacos with
  Pineapple Salsa, 106
Vegan Caesar Dressing, 52
Vegan Tzatziki, 55
garlic powder
  Baja Tofu Tacos with Citrus Crema,
    100–102
  Bang Bang Cauliflower Tacos, 88
  Buffalo Cauliflower Tacos with
    Jalapeño Ranch, 84
  Cheesy Potato Tacos, 45
  Cheesy Smashburger Tacos, 37
  Chipotle Aioli, 26
  Crispy Avocado Tacos, 130
  Crispy BBQ Cauliflower Tacos, 92
  Crispy Chickpea Tacos with Vegan
    Caesar Dressing, 52
  Delicata Squash Seeds, 134
  Grilled Tofu and Pineapple Tacos, 103–105
  Jackfruit Carnitas Tostadas, 141
  Jalapeño Popper Taquitos, 41
  Mushroom Bánh Mì–Style Tacos, 138
  Roasted Corn and Poblano Tacos, 83
  Tofu Carnitas Tacos with Apple Salsa, 118
  Vegan Burger Sauce, 37
ginger
  Coconut-Crusted Tofu Tacos, 121
  Korean-Style Tofu Tacos, 113
  Sesame Ginger Sauce, 96
  Teriyaki Tempeh Tacos with
    Pineapple Salsa, 106
gochujang
  Gochujang Sweet Potato Street Tacos, 145
  Korean-Style Tofu Tacos, 113
gold potatoes
  Cashew Queso, 24
  Cheesy Potato Tacos, 45
  Curried Potato and Cauliflower Tacos, 80
  Spicy Potato Tacos, 87

grape tomatoes: Crispy Baked
    Falafel Tacos, 63
Greek Gyro-Style Tempeh Tacos, 117
green cabbage
  Bang Bang Cauliflower Tacos, 88
  Cilantro Lime Slaw, 80
  Crispy Avocado Tacos, 130
  Sesame Slaw, 122
  Spicy Peanut Sauce, 95
Grilled Tofu and Pineapple Tacos, 103–105
Guacamole
  recipe, 20
  Sheet Pan Tofu and Fajita
    Veggie Tacos, 109

H

Hard Taco Shells
  Cheesy and Crunchy Vegan Gorditas, 46
  recipe, 18
Harissa Roasted Cauliflower
    and Chickpea Tacos, 67
hummus
  Crispy Baked Falafel Tacos, 63
  Vegan Caesar Dressing, 52

I

Impossible Ground Beef
  Cheesy and Crunchy Vegan Gorditas, 46
  Cheesy Smashburger Tacos, 37
  Chile Relleno–Style Tacos, 38

J

jackfruit
  BBQ Jackfruit Tacos, 133
  Jackfruit Carnitas Tostadas, 141
jalapeño peppers
  Apple Salsa, 118
  Avocado Corn Salsa, 71
  Baja Tofu Tacos with Citrus Crema,
    100–102
  BBQ Jackfruit Tacos, 133
  BBQ Lentil Tacos, 56
  Buffalo Cauliflower Tacos with
    Jalapeño Ranch, 84
  Crispy Baked Falafel Tacos, 63
  Grilled Tofu and Pineapple Tacos, 103–105
  Jalapeño Popper Taquitos, 41
  Jalapeño Ranch, 30
  Loaded Tater Tot Tacos, 42
  Mango Salsa, 29
  Mexican-Style Street Corn Tacos, 79
  Mushroom Bánh Mì–Style Tacos, 138
  Pineapple Salsa, 106

Salsa Roja, 23
Salsa Verde, 21
Jalapeño Ranch
  Buffalo Cauliflower Tacos with
    Jalapeño Ranch, 84
  Grilled Tofu and Pineapple Tacos, 103–105
  recipe, 30
jerk seasoning: Jerk Plantain Tacos with
    Mango Salsa, 129

K

kimchi: Korean-Style Tofu Tacos, 113
king oyster mushrooms: Mushroom Bánh
    Mì–Style Tacos, 138
Korean-Style Tofu Tacos, 113

L

Lemon Garlic Tahini Sauce, 67
lemon juice
  Cashew Queso, 24
  Greek Gyro-Style Tempeh Tacos, 117
  Lemon Garlic Tahini Sauce, 67
  Mediterranean Chickpea Tacos, 55
  Vegan Caesar Dressing, 52
  Vegan Tzatziki, 55
lemon wedges: Harissa Roasted Cauliflower
    and Chickpea Tacos, 67
lentils
  BBQ Lentil Tacos, 56
  Smoky Lentil Tacos with Avocado, 72
lettuce
  Cauliflower Walnut Tacos, 91
  Cheesy and Crunchy Vegan Gorditas, 46
  Crispy BBQ Cauliflower Tacos, 92
  Jerk Plantain Tacos with Mango Salsa, 129
  Smoky Lentil Tacos with Avocado, 72
  Vegan Burger Sauce, 37
Lime Crema, 129
lime halves: Sheet Pan Tofu and
    Fajita Veggie Tacos, 109
lime juice
  Apple Salsa, 118
  Avocado Corn Salsa, 71
  Avocado Mash, 59
  Baja Tofu Tacos with Citrus Crema,
    100–102
  Blackened Cauliflower Tacos with
    Chipotle Aioli, 76
  Cilantro Lime Slaw, 80
  Citrus Crema, 100–102
  Coconut-Crusted Tofu Tacos, 121
  Grilled Tofu and Pineapple Tacos, 103–105
  Guacamole, 20
  Jackfruit Carnitas Tostadas, 141

156 |||| THE TACO TUESDAY COOKBOOK: PLANT-BASED

Jalapeño Ranch, 30
Jerk Plantain Tacos with Mango Salsa, 129
Mango Salsa, 29
Mexican-Style Street Corn Tacos, 79
Mushroom Bánh Mì–Style Tacos, 138
Pineapple Salsa, 106
Roasted Corn and Poblano Tacos, 83
Salsa Roja, 23
Salsa Verde, 21
Sesame Slaw, 122
Spicy Mayo Sauce, 121
Spicy Peanut Sauce, 95
Teriyaki Tempeh Tacos with
   Pineapple Salsa, 106
Tostada Shells, 18
lime wedges
BBQ Jackfruit Tacos, 133
Butternut Squash and Soy
   Chorizo Tacos, 110
Cauliflower Walnut Tacos, 91
Crispy Black Bean and Cashew
   Queso Tacos, 34
Spicy Potato Tacos, 87
Sweet Potato and Black Bean Tostadas, 60
Tofu Carnitas Tacos with Apple Salsa, 118
lime zest
Chipotle Roasted Brussels
   Sprout Tacos, 146
Citrus Crema, 100–102
Grilled Tofu and Pineapple Tacos, 103–105
Jerk Plantain Tacos with Mango Salsa, 129
Roasted Corn and Poblano Tacos, 83
Loaded Tater Tot Tacos, 42

M

Mango Salsa
Jerk Plantain Tacos with Mango Salsa, 129
recipe, 29
Soy Chorizo Tacos with Mango Salsa, 114
Maple Miso Tempeh Tacos, 122
maple syrup
Buffalo Cauliflower Tacos with
   Jalapeño Ranch, 84
Chipotle Aioli, 26
Chipotle Roasted Brussels
   Sprout Tacos, 146
Coconut-Crusted Tofu Tacos, 121
Gochujang Sweet Potato Street Tacos, 145
introduction to, 12
Jackfruit Carnitas Tostadas, 141
Korean-Style Tofu Tacos, 113
Maple Miso Tempeh Tacos, 122
Maple Tahini, 134
Miso-Glazed Mushroom Tacos, 126

Mushroom Bánh Mì–Style Tacos, 138
Sesame Ginger Sauce, 96
Spicy Peanut Sauce, 95
Vegan Caesar Dressing, 52
Maple Tahini, 134
masa harina: Corn Tortillas, 16
mayo (vegan)
Bang Bang Sauce, 88
BBQ Lentil Tacos, 56
Chipotle Aioli, 26
Cilantro Lime Slaw, 80
Citrus Crema, 100–102
Mexican-Style Street Corn Tacos, 79
Spicy Mayo Sauce, 121
Sriracha Mayo, 138
Vegan Burger Sauce, 37
Mediterranean Chickpea Tacos, 55
Mexican-style cheese (vegan):
   Loaded Tater Tot Tacos, 42
Mexican-Style Street Corn Tacos, 79
milk (nondairy): Crispy Avocado Tacos, 130
mint
Harissa Roasted Cauliflower and
   Chickpea Tacos, 67
Mushroom Bánh Mì–Style Tacos, 138
miso paste
Maple Miso Tempeh Tacos, 122
Miso-Glazed Mushroom Tacos, 126
mushrooms
Miso-Glazed Mushroom Tacos, 126
Mushroom Bánh Mì–Style Tacos, 138
Roasted Portobello Mushroom Tacos, 142

N

nutritional yeast: Vegan Caesar Dressing, 52

O

olive oil
Buffalo Cauliflower Tacos with
   Jalapeño Ranch, 84
Chimichurri Grilled Veggie and
   White Bean Tacos, 68
Crispy Baked Falafel Tacos, 63
Mediterranean Chickpea Tacos, 55
onion powder
Baja Tofu Tacos with Citrus Crema,
   100–102
Bang Bang Cauliflower Tacos, 88
Cheesy Potato Tacos, 45
Cheesy Smashburger Tacos, 37
Jackfruit Carnitas Tostadas, 141
Roasted Corn and Poblano Tacos, 83
Tofu Carnitas Tacos with Apple Salsa, 118
Vegan Burger Sauce, 37

onions, crispy
Cheesy Smashburger Tacos, 37
Crispy Baked Falafel Tacos, 63
Crispy BBQ Cauliflower Tacos, 92
Vegan Burger Sauce, 37
onions, red
Apple Salsa, 118
Avocado Corn Salsa, 71
Butternut Squash and Soy
   Chorizo Tacos, 110
Greek Gyro-Style Tempeh Tacos, 117
Guacamole, 20
Mango Salsa, 29
Pickled Red Onion, 27
Pineapple Salsa, 106
onions, white
Jackfruit Carnitas Tostadas, 141
Salsa Roja, 23
Salsa Verde, 21
Soy Chorizo Tacos with Mango Salsa, 114
onions, yellow
BBQ Jackfruit Tacos, 133
BBQ Lentil Tacos, 56
Cashew Queso, 24
Crispy Baked Falafel Tacos, 63
Crispy Sheet Pan Tacos with
   Pinto Beans, 59
Pinto Bean and Avocado Corn Salsa
   Tostadas, 71
Sheet Pan Tofu and Fajita
   Veggie Tacos, 109
Smoky Lentil Tacos with Avocado, 72
Spicy Potato Tacos, 87
orange bell peppers: Sheet Pan Tofu and
   Fajita Veggie Tacos, 109
orange juice
Baja Tofu Tacos with Citrus Crema,
   100–102
BBQ Jackfruit Tacos, 133
Citrus Crema, 100–102
Jackfruit Carnitas Tostadas, 141
Tofu Carnitas Tacos with Apple Salsa, 118
orange zest: Citrus Crema, 100–102
oregano
Cheesy Smashburger Tacos, 37
Chile Relleno–Style Tacos, 38
Greek Gyro-Style Tempeh Tacos, 117
Jackfruit Carnitas Tostadas, 141
Pinto Bean and Avocado Corn
   Salsa Tostadas, 71
Tofu Carnitas Tacos with Apple Salsa, 118

INDEX **157**

P

panko breadcrumbs
Coconut-Crusted Tofu Tacos, 121
Crispy Avocado Tacos, 130

pantry, 10–13

paprika
Baja Tofu Tacos with Citrus Crema, 100–102
Bang Bang Cauliflower Tacos, 88
Cashew Queso, 24
Cheesy Potato Tacos, 45
Cheesy Smashburger Tacos, 37
Crispy Chickpea Tacos with Vegan Caesar Dressing, 52
Grilled Tofu and Pineapple Tacos, 103–105
Roasted Portobello Mushroom Tacos, 142
Smoky Butternut Squash and Apple Tacos, 137
Smoky Lentil Tacos with Avocado, 72
Spicy Plantain and Black Bean Tacos, 64
Vegan Burger Sauce, 37

parmesan cheese: Vegan Caesar Dressing, 52

parsley
Chimichurri Grilled Veggie and White Bean Tacos, 68
Delicata Squash Tacos with Maple Tahini, 134
Mediterranean Chickpea Tacos, 55

peanut butter: Spicy Peanut Sauce, 95

peanuts: Spicy Peanut Sauce, 95

pepitas: Roasted Pepitas, 137

Pickled Carrots, 138

Pickled Cucumbers, 145

Pickled Red Onion
Avocado Corn Salsa, 71
Chipotle Roasted Brussels Sprout Tacos, 146
Cilantro Lime Slaw, 80
Crispy Baked Falafel Tacos, 63
Harissa Roasted Cauliflower and Chickpea Tacos, 67
Loaded Tater Tot Tacos, 42
Maple Miso Tempeh Tacos, 122
recipe, 27
Roasted Portobello Mushroom Tacos, 142
Sweet Potato and Black Bean Tostadas, 60

pickles: Vegan Burger Sauce, 37

pico de gallo
Cauliflower Walnut Tacos, 91
Cheesy Potato Tacos, 45
Crispy Black Bean and Cashew Queso Tacos, 34

Loaded Tater Tot Tacos, 42
Smoky Lentil Tacos with Avocado, 72

pineapple
Coconut-Crusted Tofu Tacos, 121
Grilled Tofu and Pineapple Tacos, 103–105
Pineapple Salsa, 106

Pinto Bean and Avocado Corn Salsa Tostadas, 71

pinto beans
Cheesy Bean and Rice Taquitos, 49
Crispy Sheet Pan Tacos with Pinto Beans, 59
introduction to, 12
Pinto Bean and Avocado Corn Salsa Tostadas, 71

pita bread: Cheesy and Crunchy Vegan Gorditas, 46

plantains
Jerk Plantain Tacos with Mango Salsa, 129
Spicy Plantain and Black Bean Tacos, 64

poblano peppers
Chile Relleno–Style Tacos, 38
Roasted Corn and Poblano Tacos, 83
Salsa Verde, 21

pomegranate seeds: Delicata Squash Tacos with Maple Tahini, 134

portion sizes, 13

portobello mushrooms: Roasted Portobello Mushroom Tacos, 142

potatoes
Cashew Queso, 24
Cheesy Potato Tacos, 45
Curried Potato and Cauliflower Tacos, 80
Spicy Potato Tacos, 87

potatoes, sweet
Gochujang Sweet Potato Street Tacos, 145
Spicy Peanut Sweet Potato Tacos, 95
Sweet Potato and Black Bean Tostadas, 60

Q

Quick Pickled Carrots, 126
Quick Pickled Cucumbers, 145

R

radishes
Mushroom Bánh Mì–Style Tacos, 138
Spicy Plantain and Black Bean Tacos, 64

ranch dressing
Chipotle Ranch, 41
Crispy BBQ Cauliflower Tacos, 92

red bell peppers
Avocado Corn Salsa, 71
Cheesy Bean and Rice Taquitos, 49
Chimichurri Grilled Veggie and White Bean Tacos, 68

Mango Salsa, 29
Mexican-Style Street Corn Tacos, 79
Sheet Pan Tofu and Fajita Veggie Tacos, 109

red cabbage
Bang Bang Cauliflower Tacos, 88
BBQ Jackfruit Tacos, 133
Blackened Cauliflower Tacos with Chipotle Aioli, 76
Crispy Avocado Tacos, 130
Grilled Tofu and Pineapple Tacos, 103–105
Spicy Peanut Sauce, 95

red onions
Apple Salsa, 118
Avocado Corn Salsa, 71
Chipotle Roasted Brussels Sprout Tacos, 146
Cilantro Lime Slaw, 80
Crispy Baked Falafel Tacos, 63
Greek Gyro-Style Tempeh Tacos, 117
Guacamole, 20
Harissa Roasted Cauliflower and Chickpea Tacos, 67
Loaded Tater Tot Tacos, 42
Mango Salsa, 29
Maple Miso Tempeh Tacos, 122
Pickled Red Onion, 27
Pineapple Salsa, 106
Roasted Portobello Mushroom Tacos, 142
Sweet Potato and Black Bean Tostadas, 60

red peppers: Crispy Sheet Pan Tacos with Pinto Beans, 59

red wine vinegar
Chimichurri Grilled Veggie and White Bean Tacos, 68
Greek Gyro-Style Tempeh Tacos, 117
Mediterranean Chickpea Tacos, 55

relish: Vegan Burger Sauce, 37

rice vinegar
Bang Bang Sauce, 88
Gochujang Sweet Potato Street Tacos, 145
Korean-Style Tofu Tacos, 113
Maple Miso Tempeh Tacos, 122
Miso-Glazed Mushroom Tacos, 126
Mushroom Bánh Mì–Style Tacos, 138
Pickled Carrots, 138
Quick Pickled Carrots, 126
Quick Pickled Cucumbers, 145
Sesame Ginger Sauce, 96
Spicy Peanut Sauce, 95

rice, white: Cheesy Bean and Rice Taquitos, 49

Roasted Corn and Poblano Tacos, 83

Roasted Pepitas, 137

158 |||| THE TACO TUESDAY COOKBOOK: PLANT-BASED

Roasted Portobello Mushroom Tacos, 142
romaine hearts: Vegan Caesar Dressing, 52
Roma tomatoes
  Cheesy and Crunchy Vegan Gorditas, 46
  Salsa Roja, 23

S

Salsa Roja
  Cheesy Bean and Rice Taquitos, 49
  Chile Relleno–Style Tacos, 38
  recipe, 23
Salsa Verde
  Crispy Sheet Pan Tacos with
    Pinto Beans, 59
  Jackfruit Carnitas Tostadas, 141
  recipe, 21
  Sweet Potato and Black Bean Tostadas, 60
scallions
  Bang Bang Cauliflower Tacos, 88
  Gochujang Sweet Potato Street Tacos, 145
  Jalapeño Popper Taquitos, 41
  Mexican-Style Street Corn Tacos, 79
  Miso-Glazed Mushroom Tacos, 126
  Mushroom Bánh Mì–Style Tacos, 138
  Roasted Corn and Poblano Tacos, 83
  Sticky Sesame Ginger
    Cauliflower Tacos, 96
serving sizes, 13
Sesame Ginger Sauce, 96
sesame oil
  Gochujang Sweet Potato Street Tacos, 145
  Korean-Style Tofu Tacos, 113
  Maple Miso Tempeh Tacos, 122
  Miso-Glazed Mushroom Tacos, 126
  Quick Pickled Cucumbers, 145
  Sesame Ginger Sauce, 96
  Sesame Slaw, 122
sesame seeds
  Gochujang Sweet Potato Street Tacos, 145
  Maple Miso Tempeh Tacos, 122
  Miso-Glazed Mushroom Tacos, 126
  Sesame Ginger Sauce, 96
Sheet Pan Tofu and Fajita Veggie Tacos, 109
slaw
  BBQ Lentil Tacos, 56
  Cilantro Lime Slaw, 80
  Sesame Slaw, 122
Smoky Butternut Squash and
    Apple Tacos, 137
Smoky Lentil Tacos with Avocado, 72
sour cream (vegan)
  BBQ Jackfruit Tacos, 133
  Cauliflower Walnut Tacos, 91
  Cheesy and Crunchy Vegan Gorditas, 46

Cheesy Bean and Rice Taquitos, 49
Cheesy Potato Tacos, 45
Chipotle Roasted Brussels
    Sprout Tacos, 146
Citrus Crema, 100–102
Crispy Black Bean and Cashew
    Queso Tacos, 34
Loaded Tater Tot Tacos, 42
Roasted Corn and Poblano Tacos, 83
Sheet Pan Tofu and Fajita
    Veggie Tacos, 109
soy chorizo
  Butternut Squash and Soy
    Chorizo Tacos, 110
  Cashew Queso, 24
  Soy Chorizo Tacos with Mango Salsa, 114
soy sauce
  Coconut-Crusted Tofu Tacos, 121
  Gochujang Sweet Potato Street Tacos, 145
  Grilled Tofu and Pineapple Tacos, 103–105
  Korean-Style Tofu Tacos, 113
  Maple Miso Tempeh Tacos, 122
  Miso-Glazed Mushroom Tacos, 126
  Roasted Portobello Mushroom Tacos, 142
  Sesame Ginger Sauce, 96
  Smoky Lentil Tacos with Avocado, 72
  Spicy Peanut Sauce, 95
  Teriyaki Tempeh Tacos with
    Pineapple Salsa, 106
Spicy Mayo Sauce, 121
Spicy Peanut Sauce, 95
Spicy Peanut Sweet Potato Tacos, 95
Spicy Plantain and Black Bean Tacos, 64
Spicy Potato Tacos, 87
squash
  Butternut Squash and Soy
    Chorizo Tacos, 110
  Delicata Squash Seeds, 134
  Delicata Squash Tacos with
    Maple Tahini, 134
  Smoky Butternut Squash and
    Apple Tacos, 137
sriracha
  Bang Bang Sauce, 88
  Spicy Mayo Sauce, 121
  Spicy Peanut Sauce, 95
  Sriracha Mayo, 138
Sticky Sesame Ginger Cauliflower Tacos, 96
sweet chili sauce: Bang Bang Sauce, 88
sweet potatoes
  Gochujang Sweet Potato Street Tacos, 145
  Spicy Peanut Sweet Potato Tacos, 95
  Sweet Potato and Black Bean Tostadas, 60

T

taco seasoning
  Cauliflower Walnut Tacos, 91
  Cheesy and Crunchy Vegan Gorditas, 46
  Cheesy Bean and Rice Taquitos, 49
  Crispy Sheet Pan Tacos with
    Pinto Beans, 59
  Loaded Tater Tot Tacos, 42
tahini
  Lemon Garlic Tahini Sauce, 67
  Maple Tahini, 134
tamari
  Greek Gyro-Style Tempeh Tacos, 117
  Jackfruit Carnitas Tostadas, 141
  Maple Tahini, 134
  Mushroom Bánh Mì–Style Tacos, 138
  Sheet Pan Tofu and Fajita
    Veggie Tacos, 109
tater tots: Loaded Tater Tot Tacos, 42
tempeh
  Greek Gyro-Style Tempeh Tacos, 117
  Maple Miso Tempeh Tacos, 122
Teriyaki Tempeh Tacos with
    Pineapple Salsa, 106
thyme: Greek Gyro-Style Tempeh Tacos, 117
tofu
  Baja Tofu Tacos with Citrus Crema,
    100–102
  Coconut-Crusted Tofu Tacos, 121
  Korean-Style Tofu Tacos, 113
  Sheet Pan Tofu and Fajita
    Veggie Tacos, 109
  Tofu Carnitas Tacos with Apple Salsa, 118
tomatillos: Salsa Verde, 21
tomatoes, cherry
  Greek Gyro-Style Tempeh Tacos, 117
  Mediterranean Chickpea Tacos, 55
  Roasted Portobello Mushroom Tacos, 142
tomatoes, grape: Crispy Baked
    Falafel Tacos, 63
tomatoes, Roma
  Cheesy and Crunchy Vegan Gorditas, 46
  Salsa Roja, 23
tomato paste: Smoky Lentil Tacos with
    Avocado, 72
tortillas, corn
  Baja Tofu Tacos with Citrus Crema,
    100–102
  Bang Bang Cauliflower Tacos, 88
  Buffalo Cauliflower Tacos with
    Jalapeño Ranch, 84
  Butternut Squash and Soy
    Chorizo Tacos, 110
  Cauliflower Walnut Tacos, 91

INDEX   **159**

Cheesy Potato Tacos, 45
Chile Relleno–Style Tacos, 38
Chipotle Roasted Brussels
    Sprout Tacos, 146
Cilantro Lime Slaw, 80
Crispy BBQ Cauliflower Tacos, 92
Delicata Squash Tacos with
    Maple Tahini, 134
Grilled Tofu and Pineapple Tacos, 103–105
Hard Taco Shells, 18
introduction to, 12
Jerk Plantain Tacos with Mango Salsa, 129
Korean-Style Tofu Tacos, 113
recipe, 16
Roasted Portobello Mushroom Tacos, 142
Smoky Butternut Squash and
    Apple Tacos, 137
Smoky Lentil Tacos with Avocado, 72
Soy Chorizo Tacos with Mango Salsa, 114
Tofu Carnitas Tacos with Apple Salsa, 118
Tostada Shells, 18
tortillas, fajita
    Crispy Baked Falafel Tacos, 63
    Mediterranean Chickpea Tacos, 55
    Sheet Pan Tofu and Fajita
        Veggie Tacos, 109
tortillas, flour
    Baja Tofu Tacos with Citrus Crema,
        100–102
    BBQ Jackfruit Tacos, 133
    BBQ Lentil Tacos, 56
    Blackened Cauliflower Tacos
        with Chipotle Aioli, 76
    Buffalo Cauliflower Tacos
        with Jalapeño Ranch, 84
    Cheesy Bean and Rice Taquitos, 49
    Cheesy Smashburger Tacos, 37
    Chimichurri Grilled Veggie and
        White Bean Tacos, 68
    Coconut-Crusted Tofu Tacos, 121
    Crispy Avocado Tacos, 130
    Crispy Black Bean and Cashew
        Queso Tacos, 34
    Crispy Sheet Pan Tacos with
        Pinto Beans, 59
    Gochujang Sweet Potato Street Tacos, 145
    Harissa Roasted Cauliflower and
        Chickpea Tacos, 67
    introduction to, 12
    Loaded Tater Tot Tacos, 42
    Maple Miso Tempeh Tacos, 122
    Mexican-Style Street Corn Tacos, 79
    Miso-Glazed Mushroom Tacos, 126
    Mushroom Bánh Mì–Style Tacos, 138

Pineapple Salsa, 106
recipe, 19
Roasted Corn and Poblano Tacos, 83
Roasted Portobello Mushroom Tacos, 142
Spicy Peanut Sauce, 95
Spicy Potato Tacos, 87
Sticky Sesame Ginger
    Cauliflower Tacos, 96
Vegan Caesar Dressing, 52
Tostada Shells
    Avocado Corn Salsa, 71
    Jackfruit Carnitas Tostadas, 141
    recipe, 18
    Sweet Potato and Black Bean Tostadas, 60
tzatziki
    Crispy Baked Falafel Tacos, 63
    Greek Gyro-Style Tempeh Tacos, 117
    Vegan Tzatziki, 55

V

Vegan Burger Sauce, 37
Vegan Tzatziki
    Crispy Baked Falafel Tacos, 63
    Greek Gyro-Style Tempeh Tacos, 117
    recipe, 55
vegetable broth
    BBQ Lentil Tacos, 56
    Cheesy and Crunchy Vegan Gorditas, 46
    Smoky Lentil Tacos with Avocado, 72
vinegar, balsamic
    Chipotle Roasted Brussels
        Sprout Tacos, 146
    Roasted Portobello Mushroom Tacos, 142
vinegar, red wine
    Chimichurri Grilled Veggie and
        White Bean Tacos, 68
    Greek Gyro-Style Tempeh Tacos, 117
    Vegan Tzatziki, 55
vinegar, rice
    Bang Bang Sauce, 88
    Maple Miso Tempeh Tacos, 122
    Mushroom Bánh Mì–Style Tacos, 138
    Pickled Carrots, 138
    Quick Pickled Carrots, 126
    Quick Pickled Cucumbers, 145
    Sesame Ginger Sauce, 96
vinegar, white
    Pickled Red Onion, 27
    Vegan Burger Sauce, 37

W

walnuts
    Cauliflower Walnut Tacos, 91
    Smoky Lentil Tacos with Avocado, 72

white masa harina: Corn Tortillas, 16
white onions
    Jackfruit Carnitas Tostadas, 141
    Salsa Roja, 23
    Salsa Verde, 21
    Soy Chorizo Tacos with Mango Salsa, 114
white rice: Cheesy Bean and
    Rice Taquitos, 49
white vinegar
    Pickled Red Onion, 27
    Vegan Burger Sauce, 37

Y

yellow bell peppers: Sheet Pan Tofu and
    Fajita Veggie Tacos, 109
yellow masa harina: Corn Tortillas, 16
yellow onions
    BBQ Jackfruit Tacos, 133
    BBQ Lentil Tacos, 56
    Cashew Queso, 24
    Crispy Baked Falafel Tacos, 63
    Crispy Sheet Pan Tacos with
        Pinto Beans, 59
    Pinto Bean and Avocado
        Corn Salsa Tostadas, 71
    Sheet Pan Tofu and Fajita
        Veggie Tacos, 109
    Smoky Lentil Tacos with Avocado, 72
    Spicy Potato Tacos, 87
yogurt
    Jalapeño Popper Taquitos, 41
    Vegan Tzatziki, 55
Yukon gold potatoes
    Cashew Queso, 24
    Cheesy Potato Tacos, 45
    Curried Potato and Cauliflower Tacos, 80
    Spicy Potato Tacos, 87

Z

zucchini: Chimichurri Grilled Veggie and
    White Bean Tacos, 68